Hiram & Jonas
the Story of One Twin

Wendy Boyd

Christian Light Publications, Inc
Harrisonburg, Virginia 22802

HIRAM AND JONAS, THE STORY OF ONE TWIN
Christian Light Publications, Inc.,
Harrisonburg, Virginia 22802
© 2007 by Christian Light Publications, Inc.
Printed in the United States of America

2nd Printing, 2011

Cover design:
Joseph Ebersole / Illustra Graphics
Myerstown, Pennsylvania

Cover photo:
©Dreamstime.com/Pascale Wowak

Inside photos:
Courtesy of Russell and Wendy Boyd.

Footprint graphics are Hiram and Jonas's footprints at birth,
actual size.

ISBN 978-0-87813-655-1

Dedication

For Hiram, so that you will know your story.

For Jonas, so that he will not be forgotten.

Contents

Acknowledgements

First, I want to thank God. Many times I was not as diligent as I could have been, but God was faithful and allowed me to finish this book.

Thanks to my husband Russ for helping me remember, type, critique, and revise . . . and for occasionally taking the children out of the house so I could have some quiet to work.

Thanks to my children, Patience, Owen, Hiram, Quentin, and Melora, for all the times they played quietly (or napped!) while I typed.

Thanks to Leon Yoder for the patience, skill, and wisdom he exhibited in editing this book.

Thanks to our friends and family who read this book in its formative stages and made suggestions: Mom and Dad Boyd, Mom and Dad Fink, Lorinda Dexter, Dr. Cris Javier, Wilma Martin, and especially Allen Petre, who suggested that we send the book to CLP.

For privacy, some names in this account have been changed.

Foreword

August 27, 2006

Dear Hiram,

When your mother started writing this book more than three years ago, it was intended as a record for you to know everything you went through in your first tumultuous months. It has become much more. As Mommy and I worked on it, we began to realize it is also a record of our family – a record of a formative time that had incalculable influence on who we are today. While we trusted God then, we rely on Him now. While we followed God then, we seek Him now. I've sometimes wondered how we would handle the events of that summer if we faced them now, but it is those very events that have served to make us who we are now. The Lord has used your birth, your brother's death, and your struggle to survive to bring us to a place in our continuing journey that we may never have reached on an easier path. I hope you enjoy your story – our story – and I hope it helps you draw closer to the God who miraculously brought you through.

Daddy

Introduction

Dear Hiram,

As you approach your first birthday, I feel the need to record last year's events while they are still somewhat fresh in my mind. I know that someday you'll probably have a lot of questions about yourself and Jonas, so I want to lay out the story for you in chronological order. Maybe this will even evolve into the book I've dreamed of writing, and others can share your story too.

Love,

Mommy

P.S. Yesterday was Mother's Day. We took you to Jonas's grave. It was bittersweet to see you sitting on the small, still-bare patch of dirt under which lies the body of your identical twin brother.

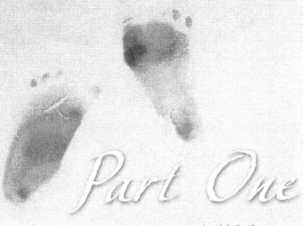

Part One

Except the LORD build the house,
they labour in vain that build it: except the LORD
keep the city, the watchman waketh but in vain.

It is vain for you to rise up early, to sit up late,
to eat the bread of sorrows: for so he giveth his beloved sleep.

Lo, children are an heritage of the LORD:
and the fruit of the womb is his reward.

As arrows are in the hand of a mighty man;
so are children of the youth.

Happy is the man that hath his quiver full of them:
they shall not be ashamed, but they
shall speak with the enemies in the gate.

Psalm 127

Chapter One

Hiram and Jonas. Identical twins. Your names are intertwined in my mind even now. Little did we know that you would never be together—that you would never even touch. Instead, you were separated by the wide gulf between Heaven and earth—one going ahead to Jesus; one left behind to live this life. Sometimes I wonder who left whom behind. It seems so strange that you and Jonas, who started as the same cell, and then split into two—are now separated into two different worlds.

When I look back on the first few months of your existence inside me, my recurring thought is that everything seemed so *normal*. How could something that seemed so normal turn out so wrong? I guess things ceased to be normal once we knew there were two of you.

Sunday, April 21, 2002.

I was just over twenty weeks pregnant, and we were excited about the upcoming ultrasound. We couldn't wait to find out if you were a girl or a boy. We planned to take

Patience (then four) and Owen (almost two) along with us so they could see their new sibling on the ultrasound screen.

This pregnancy had been pretty typical so far. My only complaint was my usual severe morning sickness. The only difference I noticed between this pregnancy and my previous two was that I was a lot bigger a lot earlier. But I wasn't concerned. This was our third baby, and I figured my abdominal muscles were worn out.

Because of my size, Grandma (my mother) was sure I was having twins. I wondered myself but refused to seriously consider the possibility. I didn't want to risk disappointment if the ultrasound revealed a single baby.

I decided to measure myself, partly to quiet Grandma's insistence about twins and partly to satisfy my own curiosity. Measuring just the way I had seen my doctors do when I was expecting Patience and Owen, I came up with 25 centimeters. It should have been 20. According to my copy of *Williams Obstetrics,* twin pregnancies at this stage typically measure about 5 centimeters more than single pregnancies.

What if Grandma were right! I shared my findings with Daddy, but didn't tell Grandma. I still didn't want to get too excited.

Monday, April 22, 2002

The next morning we hurried to leave for my ultrasound. Daddy's schedule was very flexible, allowing him to come along for all my appointments. We were both students in an intense degree program in Lancaster, PA. Daddy's classes met Monday evenings and mine on

Thursday evenings. To make up for the minimal class time, we had massive amounts of homework.

Daddy was due to graduate in less than a month. But because I had started a slightly more involved program a year behind Daddy, I would not finish until September 2003. I had planned to continue classes even after your birth. I'd joked with my classmates that unless you were born on a Wednesday or Thursday, I wouldn't have to miss a single class.

To allow us enough study time, we each had several part-time jobs rather than one full-time job. Daddy drove a large newspaper route. He was also the assistant pastor of our recently started church, Stone Hill Fellowship, where we led the youth group together. We both worked for Grandpa (my father), making home security products for his business. I also worked five hours every Saturday at a self-storage facility, taking Patience and Owen with me so that Daddy could study or work at home.

Grandma and Grandpa gave us a very cheap rent arrangement in their first-floor apartment, and our parents were paying our college tuition. This gave us a lot of flexibility without any major financial strains.

We'd been making payments to my doctors prior to my due date. We had our last payment for them with us when we arrived for my ultrasound.

There were two doctors in the practice, Dr. Anthony Rosato, and Dr. Sarah Davis. Patients alternated between the two doctors for their visits. Dr. Rosato had done all my previous ultrasounds and had delivered both Patience and

Owen. We were considerably more attached to him and were glad he was doing the ultrasound. A man of few words, he had a quiet, unreadable manner that I had initially found hard to get used to; but we'd built up a rapport with him over the past few years.

Dr. Rosato had the ultrasound on my abdomen for only a few seconds before he got a quiet smile on his face. He looked up and said simply, "It's twins."

Even though I'd suspected it, I was still shocked. Few parents ever experience having twins. I couldn't believe we would be among the few to be so blessed. Daddy was less surprised because he'd seen two babies on the screen before Dr. Rosato told us. Patience didn't seem taken aback at all. "Well, Grandma sure was right!" she chirped. "There *are* two babies in there!"

Dr. Rosato first looked at Baby A (this was you, Hiram) on my right side and identified you as a boy. I'd really thought we were having a girl. *Oh, well,* I thought, *maybe Baby B is a girl.* Pop Pop (Daddy's father) thought we were having a girl, and Mom Mom (Daddy's mother) thought we were having a boy. I could already imagine calling Daddy's parents to tell them they were both right and letting them puzzle it out.

Finished with Baby A, Dr. Rosato swung the ultrasound to my left side to examine Baby B (Jonas). Baby B was also a boy. Mom Mom was doubly right.

After the ultrasound, we all met in Dr. Rosato's office so he could explain the implications of a twin gestation. He said there was an increased risk of preterm labor and delivery, especially after week twenty-eight when I would be the same size as that of a full-term single pregnancy. Twins also have an increased risk of birth defects. Because of that, Dr. Rosato routinely recommended that patients with twins have a level-two ultrasound. He added that he'd gotten a pretty good look at all the major organs during the ultrasound, and it was completely up to us.

We decided not to.

Chapter Two

At his class that night, Daddy told his classmates our news. His professor was a twin with two older siblings. His sisters had been ages 6 and 12 when he and his brother were born.

"How old are your two other children?" the professor asked Daddy.

"Two and four," Daddy told him.

"The Lord bless you," said the professor.

Tuesday, April 23, 2002

I had had no doubts about my ability to keep up with Patience, Owen, a newborn, and class. But *two* newborns was something else.

I had wanted so badly to complete my degree. When Daddy and I decided I should withdraw from school, I cried. In spite of morning *and* evening sickness, I hadn't missed a single class. I had been *so* determined to finish.

I could have planned to continue until August, just to complete a few more classes, but I was quite large already and having severe back pain when I sat for long periods. Classes lasted four hours—from six to ten p.m. I figured that since I wasn't going to complete my degree anyway, I might as well quit now rather than suffer.

When I told Penny, my manager at the self-storage, that we were expecting twins, she asked how I would manage my job *and* a set of twins. With seven-year-old twin boys, she knew firsthand how difficult it was to care for a set of twins.

I had just decided to give up college. It hadn't even occurred to me that I'd need to give up my job too—until I talked to Penny. Daddy and I talked it over and decided I should quit my job also. I made plans to work for a few more weeks.

Wednesday, April 24, 2002

Feeling overwhelmed at the idea of twins, and also feeling a bit sorry for myself at having to give up my job and my education, I walked around the yard trying to find some peace. Grandma had Patience and Owen; and Daddy was in the barn (where Grandpa had all his equipment set up) making products for Grandpa's business. I sent him a text message:

In yard. Almost
ready to cry.
Feeling
overwhelmed at
the idea of
twins.

After a few moments I updated him with another text
message:

> Still in yard.
> Crying.

Daddy replied:

> Children are a
> gift from the
> Lord :) :)

And then he came out to comfort me. I still have his
message on my phone.

It only took me a few days to adjust to the idea of two of
you. Being blessed with twins was so special that I no longer
minded not finishing my degree and having to quit my job.
It was still overwhelming to think of two preschoolers and
two newborns. Our number of children would *double* when
you boys were born, but we looked forward to having twins.
How many couples ever experience something that special?
And you were *identical* twins, no less.

Thursday, April 25, 2002

I arrived early to class to inform my professor of my
withdrawal and to say good-bye to classmates I'd grown
close to. I left just before class began.

I was sorry not to see Karen. Every week since she knew
I was pregnant, she had teasingly asked, "How are the
twins?" I had been looking forward to seeing her reaction
when I answered her, "The twins are both just fine."

But as the next few weeks passed, I began to wonder if the twins really were fine. I grew noticeably bigger *every day*. I knew I'd be bigger with twins; but even taking twins into account, this seemed excessive.

Meanwhile, Daddy and I needed to think about names. We had a girl's name chosen, but no boy's name. Now we had to come up with names for *two* boys. I suggested at one point that we could name you Gary Bruce Boyd (after Pop Pop) and name your brother Jeffrey Lee Boyd (after Grandpa). Daddy said no. He liked the concept, but we didn't like the way the names flowed.

We wanted your names to have the same feel without sounding "twinny." We didn't want names that rhymed or started with the same letter. We didn't even plan on dressing you the same. We wanted you and Jonas to have separate identities. We had no idea how separate those identities would be.

We looked through several name books before deciding on first names. We chose to name one of you Hiram, which means "exalted one" in Hebrew, and to call the other Jonas, which means "dove." Both are Bible names and have an old-fashioned, Civil-War-Era feel to them.

Maybe you wonder how we decided which name to give to which twin. You seemed to be more active, and we thought the name *Hiram* seemed more suitable for you. *Jonas* seemed to better fit a quieter type like your brother. I could already picture the two of you getting into mischief together, with you as the ringleader.

I was a little hesitant about Jonas's name. I knew twins

have a much higher mortality rate than singletons. As I thought about giving Jonas a name that meant "dove," I hoped it wouldn't mean that he would fly away from us to Heaven. Almost as soon as the thought entered my mind, I pushed it away without even telling Daddy about my foolishness.

We chose your middle names based more on meaning than on the way they sounded. Your middle name would be *Joseph*. When Rachel in the Old Testament had her first child after years of barrenness, she named him Joseph, which means, "he shall add." She chose the name because God was finally adding to her family by giving her Joseph. God was certainly adding to our family too, by giving us twins, so the name seemed appropriate. We used the same reasoning in choosing *Nathaniel* as Jonas's middle name. Nathaniel means "God's gracious gift." The Bible says in Psalm 127 that children are a gift from the Lord. God was giving us quite a gift by blessing us with two children at once.

Tuesday, May 7, 2002

About two weeks after my ultrasound, I measured myself again, at Grandma's insistence. I asked her to measure me too, to see how our measurements compared. A large abdomen does not always indicate a large uterus; it could just be a case of slack abdominal muscles. I wanted some exact numbers to go by.

Grandma measured 36 centimeters, and I measured 35: a ten-centimeter gain in two weeks. With a single pregnancy, a mother would expect growth of about one centimeter per week. I'd grown five times that, which seemed excessive, even for twins. I worried that I might have too much amniotic fluid. And I was also experiencing an increasing, severe pain in my ribs—in the front and in the back.

I hated to call the doctors about my concerns for fear they would think I was bothering them for no good reason. With Grandma beside me for encouragement, I dialed the doctor's office. When I explained the reason for my call, Sue, the office manager, chuckled, knowing I was expecting twins. I did feel extremely foolish. I was carrying twins and calling to tell my doctor I was too big and was concerned about excess amniotic fluid. Of course I was big!

Sue humored me and had Dr. Rosato call me back. His response included three elements: 1) you can't measure yourself, 2) measurements don't mean anything in a twin pregnancy anyway, and 3) they'd be checking my amniotic fluid volume at a later date. To relieve my back pain, he recommended a prenatal cradle, a kind of support belt to ease the pressure of a large abdomen.

In closing he said, "You have to understand—with twins, this is not going to be easy."

Grandma had stayed with me during the entire conversation. When I got off the phone, she comforted me while I cried. I was crying because I thought I might be *wrong,* and I'd bothered Dr. Rosato about something totally foolish; and I was crying because I thought I might be *right,* and I couldn't get my doctor to seriously consider my concerns.

Wednesday, May 8, 2002

Owen had his annual checkup with our family doctor today. Seeing my pain, Daddy insisted on coming along. His classes had just ended, and he had yet to find a full-time job, so he had extra time to help me out. When Dr. Buczewski (boo CHESS key) saw me, he seemed surprised at how big I was. He'd seen me about six weeks before when I'd brought Patience in for her annual checkup.

"When are you due?" he asked again, looking at me thoughtfully.

I told him the date was September 6, and hastened to explain that we were having twins.

"Well, it doesn't look like you're putting on the weight anywhere else, anyway," he commented. "Who's your OB?"

"Rosato and Davis."

"Well, I guess they're taking good care of you," he said.

I was tempted to share my concerns with him, but didn't want to be seen as playing one doctor against another. Besides, since obstetrics was not Dr. Buczewski's area of expertise, I doubted he would feel comfortable giving an opinion. So I kept silent.

Dr. Buczewski turned his attention to Owen. Everything was fine, something I would no longer take for granted with our children by the end of the summer.

Throughout the week my pain and abdominal size increased so that I could do little more than sit in the recliner leaned back at a forty-five degree angle. Even that didn't eliminate the pain, but only made it tolerable. I was still concerned that something might be wrong with this pregnancy.

I would have done some research on the Internet, but it hurt too much to sit in front of the computer.

I had made baby quilts for Patience and Owen before they were born, and I wanted to make quilts for you and Jonas also. But I couldn't start two baby quilts in my condition. They would have to wait until after you were born.

There wasn't much I *could* do with the pain I was in. I couldn't get up to discipline Patience and Owen. I couldn't cook my own meals, let alone sit at the table to eat them.

I felt like all I could do was be a baby incubator. But even then, I knew this was a very important job. I'd read stories about preemies and all the medical technology necessary to keep them alive, when a few more weeks inside the mother would have done a better job. I also knew that being a patient in a neonatal intensive care unit (NICU, pronounced "nick you") had to be an awful experience for a baby.

I used this knowledge to steel myself to endure the rest of the summer. Any mother would take pain for her children if she could. I told myself that was what I was doing. You and Jonas weren't ready to be born anytime soon. If you did, your condition would be very painful and precarious; you would probably both die or be disabled. I was ready to go the distance, even if I lost my sanity in the process. Many times after your birth, I wished you were both back inside me, alive and well.

Daddy would graduate that coming weekend. The baccalaureate would be Friday night and the commencement Saturday afternoon. But my pain was so severe, that I didn't know how I would make it through the ceremonies.

Chapter Three

Friday, May 10, 2002

I took lots of pillows with me for Daddy's baccalaureate. I probably looked like a beached whale, leaning against all those pillows. I already looked bigger than when I'd delivered Patience or Owen. I felt foolish carrying all those pillows; but my desperation overcame my self-consciousness.

I don't remember much about what the speaker said that night, except that he mentioned the uncertainty of life. His comment made the audience glance around the auditorium and wonder who might not be here next week. I tended to look at the gray heads, never dreaming it would be one of my own unborn sons. As upset as I'd been by Dr. Rosato's dismissive response to my concerns, I did feel reassured that you two were okay.

As I pondered a seemingly endless summer of increasing size and pain, I remember saying, "I know my body can do it, but I don't know if my mind can do it." It never occurred to me that my body *couldn't* do it. I was more concerned about my mental health at this point than about the welfare of you and Jonas. I'd heard of post-partum depression; I began wondering if I was at risk for *pre*-partum depression.

I got through baccalaureate okay — only an hour-and-a-half. Tomorrow would be the real test of endurance — the three-hour commencement.

Saturday, May 11, 2002

Daddy didn't have to be at school for the graduation until noon, so we did some morning yard-sale shopping while Grandma watched Patience and Owen. I knew we'd need extra boy clothes and other baby items. I also knew that this might be the last Saturday I would be physically able to go.

I'd been scheduled to work my last day at the self-storage today, but Penny had said I could cancel if I wanted to, so I did.

Less than half a mile from home was a large community yard sale, and one place had lots of baby clothes. They also had some preemie clothes, which I bought knowing that you two might be a tad early and, perhaps, a tad small.

At another sale I bought two pairs of denim shortalls, sized twelve to eighteen months. One had blue and pale yellow stripes and one was plain blue — just similar enough to be cute, but still easy to tell apart. The striped pair would be for you and the plain pair for Jonas. Since you seemed to be the more colorful of our twins, we'd give you the more colorful of the two.

The last item we bought was a bunk bed, made of steel

tubing and painted a bold blue. It had a double bed on the bottom and a twin size on top. In a few years, Owen could bunk on the top and you and Jonas could share the full-size bottom bunk. It would be perfect for our three boys. We barely fit the bed frame into our Dodge Caravan. I couldn't recline my seat the way I needed to manage the pain, but at least it was a short drive home.

Once there, Daddy changed clothes and left for graduation. Grandma helped with Patience and Owen until it was time for us to leave. A family friend came to watch Patience and Owen, and I rode out to the graduation with Grandma and Grandpa.

Once again, I came armed with pillows. Somehow, I managed to get through it. Afterward, we went outside for pictures. I don't know which was worse — sitting through the commencement service, or standing for the pictures. The photos reveal a weary look on my face, but are too washed-out to do justice to the size of my abdomen.

After the pictures Daddy's parents took us out to eat. The restaurant was short staffed, so we waited almost an hour for our food. Sitting was agony without my pillows. It felt like my abdominal muscles were being ripped from their tendons. I found that leaning forward with my forearms on the table and resting my abdomen on my thighs helped relieve some of the pain.

We finally headed home around 7:00 p.m. I began having regular, painless contractions about five minutes apart, so when we got home, I called my doctors' office. Dr. Davis said I was probably slightly dehydrated since I had no pain, vomiting, or diarrhea. But, she said, if any of those symptoms should appear, that I should call again as it might be a sign of true preterm labor.

Her explanation seemed likely, because I had drunk very little that day. So I thanked Dr. Davis, got off the phone, and drank some water.

I'd also noticed a decline in your movement, but didn't bother mentioning it. When I'd mentioned similar declines with Patience and Owen, I'd been told not to worry as long as I felt ten good movements a day. I was still getting at least ten movements a day with you, so I let it pass. Plus, I'd already been calling with other concerns and didn't want to come across as an alarmist worrying about every detail of the pregnancy.

Looking back now, I should have mentioned the change. It would have seemed unusual to have one twin moving a lot less *as compared to the other*. But I'd been well trained in my first two pregnancies to believe that everything was normal (and things were indeed normal both times). Yet I wonder now if that complaint would have sounded the alarm. None of us had any idea that tomorrow would begin my final week of pregnancy.

Sunday, May 12, 2002, Mother's Day

Even with my pillows, I couldn't make it through church. I stayed long enough for Daddy's opening prayer for items highlighted on our prayer list. He also prayed for me as he had done at every Saturday evening prayer meeting and every Sunday morning since we'd known we were

having twins: "Lord, please help Wendy through this pregnancy, and help her to carry our babies as long as necessary
and not a day longer."

I couldn't make it through Pastor Dean's hour-long
sermon. I went to the room where Dean's wife had the children for children's church. It had a nice sofa where I could
lie on my side to relieve some of the pain in my ribs.

Later in the day, we all went to Great Mom Mom and
Great Pop Pop's (Grandpa's parents) house for Mother's
Day. My grandparents' enclosed patio had one lounge chair,
and my great-aunt Romaine was sitting on it when we
arrived. Daddy simply asked her to find another seat
because his pregnant wife needed the lounge chair. I was
still outside when Daddy did this. When I found out later
what he'd done, I was both horrified and grateful. I really
did need that lounge chair. The back was at a forty-five-
degree angle, and that's what I needed to tolerate the pain.

Daddy gave me a Mother's Day card with all *four* children's names signed on it. We signed the cards for our moth-
ers the same way. I still have my card. I know it's the only
card I'll ever get with *both* your name and Jonas's name on it.

Tuesday, May 14, 2002

For the last week or so, I'd been sleeping on the sofa,
lying on my side with my back against the sofa back. That
extra support lessened my pain enough that I could sleep.
But now, even the sofa didn't alleviate the pain, so I started
sleeping on the recliner. I already spent all day sitting on the
recliner while Grandma cared for Patience and Owen. Now I

was spending all night there too. And the pain was still horrible. I used heating pads on my abdomen and back, which helped take a little of the edge off of the pain. The pain of my abdominal muscles was now more severe than my labor pains had been with my first two deliveries.

I called the doctor's office and told this to Dr. Rosato. I reminded him of my high tolerance for pain (I had done both of my deliveries with no pain meds). I wanted to persuade him that if Wendy Boyd complained about pain, it must be serious.

He said he thought this was still in the normal range for a twin pregnancy. I asked if he could at least give me something for the pain. I'd been trying Tylenol and it made *no* difference. He said he could prescribe nothing that would be safe for a pregnant woman.

His final comment was, "This pregnancy's really bringing you to your knees, isn't it?"

It seemed harsh, but I believe he meant it compassionately. No doctor likes to see his patient in pain.

I appreciated his sympathy, but still felt my concerns weren't being taken seriously. I suspected I had one of three possible complications: too much amniotic fluid, triplets, or a fast-growing abdominal tumor. I wasn't convinced that it was normal to be this big even with twins. I got off the phone feeling brushed off again.

About five minutes later, the phone rang. It was Sue from Dr. Rosato's office. Dr. Rosato had changed his mind and wanted to see me. Daddy took me over while Grandma kept Patience and Owen.

When we got to the office, Sue looked at me and said, "Oh, you don't look *that* big!" She seemed to be making light of my concerns. Who was she to say if I looked normal or not? I just smiled and didn't answer.

We didn't wait long before Dr. Rosato came in. "Our conversation . . ." he paused, searching for words, ". . . bothered me."

He measured me at 37 centimeters and listened to both heartbeats. He said he thought the pain was all musculoskeletal, and that my extremely large uterus was actually pushing out on my ribs. I was 5 feet 6 inches with a non-pregnant weight of about 120 pounds. That's a small frame to be carrying twins. So maybe it *was* normal to feel so much pain.

"Does *every* expectant mother of twins feel this way?" I asked. I knew some women, including Penny at the self-storage, who'd had twins; and I had never heard such horror stories.

He answered, "Yeah, they're all just miserable."

I was disappointed that he didn't get out the ultrasound just to see what was going on. But I figured if he said it's normal, it must be normal. None of us had any idea what imminent danger you and Jonas were in.

More than ever now, Daddy and I were looking forward to my appointment on Friday. I was scheduled for a special ultrasound to assess my risk for preterm delivery. This was standard procedure with twins.

We also had plans to go to "the cottage" in the mountains of central Pennsylvania for the weekend. We'd gone there for our honeymoon and every anniversary since. May 20 would be our seventh anniversary.

Our senior pastor, Dean Ross, had agreed to cover Daddy's responsibilities at church, and Daddy found someone to fill in for his paper route.

Patience and Owen loved the cottage and looked forward to going. I didn't know how I could tolerate the three-and-a-half-hour drive, but I was determined.

Thursday, May 16, 2002

Daddy and I went to a surgical supply store for something similar to the prenatal cradle that Dr. Rosato had recommended — a very wide elastic belt that fastened with Velcro and went across my lower back and under my abdomen.

It was wonderful. My abdomen still hurt, but now I could at least tolerate it. I felt like I'd been given a new lease on my sanity. Walking had become very difficult, but now I walked all over our apartment. I still had a lot of pain. Halfway through lunch the pain from sitting made me retreat to the recliner. After ten minutes to get the pain under control and relax my abdominal muscles, I went to finish lunch.

With me in such a condition, Daddy felt uneasy about going to the cottage so far from home. I protested because I didn't want to disappoint Patience and Owen, but Daddy was adamant. As bad as I felt, I had to agree; but it was hard, knowing that the rest of the family had to give up their vacation on account of me.

Later in the afternoon we went to Mom Mom and Pop

Pop's house for supper. They live about 45 minutes from our home, and the drive was really painful for me. I felt like the maternity belt was already losing its effectiveness. I couldn't even sit at the table for supper. Pop Pop brought my plate to me as I reclined on the sofa. I was in such pain that I could hardly eat.

On the way home, I told Daddy that I couldn't take any more trips to his parents' home. Until this pregnancy was over, they would have to come to visit us. As it turned out, this wouldn't even be an issue. We spent the very next Thursday in their community again — for Jonas's funeral.

Part Two

Whither shall I go from thy spirit?
or whither shall I flee from thy presence?

If I ascend up into heaven, thou art there:
if I make my bed in hell,
behold, thou art there.

Psalm 139:7, 8

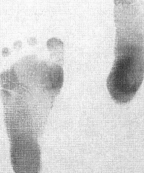

Chapter Four

That night I could not sleep because of the excruciating pain. And then I began vomiting. I didn't know at first if the vomiting meant anything since I'd never completely gotten over the morning sickness. Yet this didn't feel like morning sickness.

Friday, May 17, 2002

Around three o'clock in the morning I began noticing contractions. At first it just felt like abdominal tightening—no pain. But as I began to pay attention, I realized the contractions were indeed painful. I had so much pain anyway that it was hard to tell.

I began paying careful attention. Every time I felt that squeezing sensation, I poked to see if my abdomen was hard. This method wasn't very accurate because my abdomen was already a lot firmer with this pregnancy than it had been with my previous two. I didn't know it then, but the firm belly was a symptom of Twin-to-Twin Transfusion Syndrome that you and Jonas would later be diagnosed with.

The contractions seemed to be about five minutes apart. Finally, around 6 a.m., I decided to call my doctors.

Dr. Davis called back this time. After describing my symptoms, she said she thought they were probably due to the stomach bug or food poisoning.

"Did you eat anything unusual yesterday?" she wanted to know.

"I ate what everyone else ate and none of them got sick," I answered. Besides, I hadn't eaten *any* of the meat, which would have been the most likely source of food poisoning.

"It must be the stomach bug then," she said. "Throwing up is no fun, so if this is still going on by the time the office opens at nine, give us a call and we'll phone in a suppository prescription to the pharmacy for you."

I said okay, and we hung up; but I was puzzled. Last Saturday she had said that if I had any vomiting, diarrhea, and *painful* contractions, in addition to the painless contractions, it might be true preterm labor. So now I called with almost all of those symptoms, and she told me it was the stomach bug. Too miserable to dwell on it, I once again figured that the doctors must be right – and I stopped paying attention to the contractions.

I hadn't awakened Daddy with any of this. It was bad enough that one of us was losing a night's sleep. He had already slept on the living room couch for most of the night to keep me company; but he'd slept so soundly that he hadn't noticed my trips to the bathroom.

Daylight finally came, and the nausea slacked off some. Daddy brought me some ice chips to suck on. Today would have been our first day of vacation, so he was able to stay with me all day. I don't know how I ever would have managed without Grandma's help, but I was so glad to have Daddy for a few days. When I was this miserable, all I wanted was Daddy.

The abdominal pain was especially bad. I tried every position I could think of—even kneeling on the floor in front of the recliner.

Patience and Owen went outside with Grandma and Grandpa to play for a while. Around eleven o'clock I joined them, sitting on the steps that led up to my parents' second-floor deck. I really needed a change of scenery, and I was in pain no matter where I sat anyway.

It was Grandpa's birthday, but I don't think I even remembered to say anything to him.

Patience and Owen brought me some mint leaves, "because you're not feeling good, Mommy." I thanked them and chewed on the mint leaves. A few minutes later, Patience brought me a bunch of buttercups.

I'd forgotten this was buttercup season. The flowers reminded me of one of our wedding pictures, taken almost seven years before. A woman who lived next door to the church where we were married had been getting ready to mow her yard. Our photographer had run over to ask her if she could wait a few hours so we could get pictures at her birch tree, surrounded by a carpet of the yellow flowers. The woman agreed, and the pictures are in our album now.

We'd come a long way since then—two children, and two more on the way. Daddy put the bunch of buttercups in a vase on the kitchen table for me.

I went back inside for more miserable wandering, trying to find a comfortable position. I was so frustrated and in so much pain that I wanted to cry, but crying made my ribs and abdomen hurt even more.

Closer to noon, I vomited again — really wretched-tasting green stuff. I figured it was green because of the mint leaves I'd been chewing on, but I should have known that a couple of mint leaves would not have done that much. I'd held off calling the doctors' office about a suppository prescription since I hadn't vomited, but now I asked Daddy to call. I didn't try calling because I was afraid I'd have to throw up while I was on the phone.

Dr. Rosato decided against the prescription. In his experience, women did just as well without the suppository as with it. He simply instructed me not to take anything, not even ice chips, unless it had been at least six hours since my last episode of vomiting.

When Daddy asked if we should still come in for the ultrasound, he replied, "No! Give the poor girl a break." Then he asked to talk to me. I reluctantly agreed. He asked if I had any other complaints. I told him my lower abdomen and upper thighs were really achy. I didn't mention contractions because I wasn't noticing any at this time. Besides, I assumed Dr. Davis would have filled him in.

When I asked about my appointment, he replied firmly, "The ultrasound can wait. You need to be home in bed."

I wanted to argue, but didn't. I figured he thought I was contagious and didn't want me infecting him or his other patients. I was devastated by the cancellation. It was one thing to be called in for an unplanned visit as had happened Tuesday, but this was a pre-scheduled appointment—for an ultrasound, no less! I felt a nagging in the back of my mind that all this vomiting and the earlier contractions might be symptoms of preterm labor. As sick as I was, it seemed the perfect day to have this ultrasound, because we'd see for sure what was going on. Then Dr. Rosato canceled it. I wondered why we'd bothered calling. I *hadn't* gotten my suppository prescription, and I *had* gotten my appointment canceled.

I spent the rest of the afternoon wracked in pain and sick to my stomach. I wandered from one part of the house to another, trying to find a place to recline where I could minimize the pain. Obeying Dr. Rosato's instructions, I lay down on the bed. As bad as my pain was, I didn't think it could get any worse. Trying to lie on the bed proved me wrong.

Although I was too miserable to care about anything, I managed to summon enough concern later that afternoon to check for contractions again. I started poking my abdomen regularly to feel for contractions. I also tried to determine if I felt any additional pain and tightness. I concluded that I was indeed still, or once again, experiencing contractions, so I called the doctors' office again at 5:30 p.m.

I was really beginning to feel like a pest.

Five minutes after leaving my message with the answering service, the phone rang. Daddy jumped to answer it, thinking it must be Dr. Rosato. It wasn't. It was a wrong number.

At 6:15 p.m., after waiting forty-five minutes for Dr. Rosato to call back, Daddy went to get the phone to call again. That's when he noticed the red light flashing on the phone, indicating that we had voice mail. It was Dr. Rosato. Apparently, he had called just as Daddy was answering the wrong number. A few seconds sooner, and we would have gotten Dr. Rosato's call *before* the wrong number. A few seconds later and we would have gotten a beep for the call waiting. Sometimes I wonder if that forty-five minute delay made a difference.

We promptly called the doctor's office again, and got the answering service. Dr. Rosato called back within minutes. I told him how I was feeling, and he seemed to be hemming and hawing about sending me to the hospital.

"Try drinking some water and see if that stops the contractions," he suggested.

"You told me not to drink anything unless it's been at least six hours since I vomited," I reminded him. "It hasn't been that long yet."

"Try to drink a little something anyway."

Daddy was beside me and could tell the conversation wasn't going well. His eyebrows knit together as he looked at me. I knew that look. He wanted me to be persistent with Dr. Rosato and get myself sent to the hospital. Daddy told me later that he was ready to grab the phone and talk to Dr. Rosato himself if Dr. Rosato didn't listen to me.

I hated arguing with my doctor, but Daddy's intense look gave me a dose of courage. I took a deep breath and told Dr. Rosato that the way I felt reminded me of when I'd gone into labor with Patience. At this point he said I could go to the hospital. He said he'd be in later that night anyway and he might see me if I was still there.

I felt foolish having twisted his arm to go to the hospital. I'd go, get examined, be declared fine, and be sent home. Of course I hoped I *would* be sent home with nothing wrong, but I knew I'd feel stupid for insisting something was wrong.

Grandma and Grandpa readily agreed to keep Patience and Owen while Daddy drove me to the hospital. I brought two pillows to prop myself with, and a bowl in case I vomited. I didn't expect to be admitted, so I didn't pack anything else. I thought that even if I was in labor, they'd probably keep me for no more than a week or two to get things calmed down, and then send me home on bed rest.

As glad as we were that I was going to be examined, we were unconcerned to a certain degree. Rather than fret over our babies, I idly noticed things going by outside my window as Daddy drove — like the big stack of railroad ties next to the tracks. It looked like they were planning some repairs on the rail bed.

When we arrived at the maternity ward, the nurses seemed unconcerned as they took my history.

"She's been vomiting, which is probably why she's contracting," one nurse remarked casually as she fastened the fetal monitors around my abdomen.

A tall, slim resident came in to examine me. Dr. Metzgar was very kind, thorough, and sympathetic. When she had finished, she told me that I *was* having real contractions and that I was 4 centimeters dilated and 80 percent effaced.

Chapter Five

The atmosphere in the room instantly changed. Everyone turned serious. Dr. Metzgar started a magnesium sulfate IV to try to stop the contractions. A nurse gave me a steroid shot to mature your lungs. Since I had already vomited twice since arriving, I asked for some nausea medication. Dr. Metzgar put that in my IV as well. She also did an ultrasound, which showed a huge excess of amniotic fluid in your sac and no fluid in Jonas's. Then she called Dr. Rosato.

Strangely, at this point the rib pain seemed to be receding, and I began to really feel the contractions. Dr. Rosato sensed that when he came into my room and observed me. He asked, "You're really starting to feel the contractions now, aren't you?" I nodded mutely; I was too scared to speak.

I had just reached twenty-four weeks of pregnancy. A full-term pregnancy is forty weeks. I knew that twenty-four is generally regarded as the threshold of viability. I had read that babies born before twenty-four weeks *don't* survive; babies born *at* twenty-four weeks *might* survive; babies born just two weeks later at twenty-six weeks have a 90 percent chance of survival.

After conferring with Dr. Metzgar and seeing the ultrasound images, Dr. Rosato explained that you and Jonas had Twin-to-Twin Transfusion Syndrome (TTTS), a condition in which one twin pumps blood to the other through a shared placenta.

I'd read about TTTS in *Williams Obstetrics*. I knew it was bad. Identicals' blood vessels often connect in the placenta. An artery-to-artery connection or vein-to-vein connection doesn't cause problems because the blood flow remains equalized between the twins. TTTS happens when one twin's artery connects to the other's vein. The donor twin (the twin pumping blood to the other) is often the smaller of the two and, of course, has a lower blood volume. As the TTTS progresses, the recipient can face death due to an over-taxed heart and/or kidneys. Even in the early stages of TTTS, the recipient twin often has a huge excess of amniotic fluid while the donor twin is "stuck" with none.

Jonas was the donor twin and you were the recipient. Your amniotic fluid volume had been increasing drastically over the past few weeks, and Jonas's had decreased until he had no fluid left.

Dr. Rosato told us that a perinatologist would come shortly to get permission to do a procedure that might help. When Dr. Neubert arrived, he explained that although there were risks for you and Jonas if you stayed inside me as the TTTS progressed, our objective right now was to stop the labor. At this point, you were a lot more likely to die from prematurity than from TTTS.

TTTS is very complicated when it starts so early in a pregnancy: the earlier the twins are delivered, the greater the chance of death or disability due to prematurity; but the longer the twins remain in the mother, the greater the chance that the worsening TTTS will kill them. It's almost a no-win situation.

Dr. Neubert told us my overextended uterus had probably triggered the preterm labor. Draining some of the excess fluid from your sac might relieve some of the pressure and help stop the labor. Then he would continue monitoring you and Jonas via ultrasound to make sure the TTTS wasn't progressing to a deadly stage.

There was about a 5 percent chance that the amniocentesis could actually trigger continued labor; but the odds weighed heavily in favor of doing the procedure. Daddy signed the consent form.

I could hardly believe it. I had been concerned about excess amniotic fluid. And now your very lives were being threatened by it.

With Daddy by my side, they wheeled me to Dr. Neubert's office. Another female OB resident held the ultrasound transducer to guide Dr. Neubert throughout the reduction procedure. Dr. Neubert injected some lidocaine into my skin before carefully slipping in the needle to drain the fluid. He also poked holes in the membrane separating you and Jonas to allow the amniotic fluid to equalize between your sacs — all the while watching the needle and you and Jonas on the ultrasound screen.

I had to lie perfectly still on my back while Dr. Neubert worked—no small task as the labor pains intensified. He made five passes with the needle. Between passes, I curled up on my side to get some respite from the pain. The lidocaine made me woozy and sleepy, which helped. I almost felt as though I was in another world. A part of me wanted to stay fully alert. I wanted to see you and Jonas on the ultrasound screen, knowing this might be the last I would see you alive, yet it was so much easier to lie still when I let myself drift into "lidocaineland." I decided to let myself drift, partly to conserve the energy I knew I would need, and partly to ensure that I would be as still as possible so that no additional harm would come to my boys while Dr. Neubert delicately maneuvered the needle around you both.

Daddy was absorbed with the ultrasound screen. He said it was incredible to watch Dr. Neubert at work. Within minutes Jonas was swimming freely again.

I was aware enough to feel my abdomen deflating as Dr. Neubert drained off amniotic fluid. Oh, the relief! I couldn't believe how wonderful it felt to be rid of that excess fluid.

Dr. Neubert asked a resident to collect the fluid as it drained so it could be measured, but several times it gushed out of the needle like a geyser before she could attach a vial. Dr. Neubert estimated that he drained about one liter. The entire procedure lasted about two hours.

When Dr. Neubert was done, the nurse wheeled me to a different room—one of the high-risk OB rooms. I wondered how long we would be in it. They said it would take forty-eight hours for the steroids to have optimum effect on your lungs, and at least twenty-four before any effect would begin. I hoped they could hold off labor at least that long. Maybe my labor would stop altogether.

In a nearby room, Daddy updated Grandma via text messaging from a cell phone. Grandma stayed up all night calling people, waking them out of their sleep to pray.

Saturday, May 18, 2002

I was to notify the nurse if I felt pain with my contractions, and they would increase the dosage of the magnesium sulfate that was to stop my labor. Every time they increased the drug, the pain stopped for a while, but the contractions kept intensifying and they would have to increase it again. They'd increased it so much that they decided to do a blood test to make sure the level wasn't high enough to be toxic.

Before they got a chance, I buzzed for the nurse because something felt strange. Dr. Metzgar examined me and found that I was now 6 centimeters dilated and 100 percent effaced. There was no stopping the labor now, so they discontinued the drug. I hadn't thrown up since I had first arrived at the hospital, but now I was so upset that I almost vomited again.

They still wanted me to lie on my back to hold off the delivery as long as possible. I hadn't been allowed pain meds before this, because I had needed to feel the contractions. I'd done my first two deliveries with no pain medication, but I'd been allowed to sit, walk, take a shower, or do whatever was necessary to manage the pain. I found myself propping up my elbow ever so slightly to deal with the pain.

Knowing that I really needed to stay *flat*, I asked for an epidural.

While we waited for the anesthesiologist to arrive, Dr. Gerard Brown came to my room and introduced himself as the neonatologist (baby doctor) on call. As kindly and gently as possible, he told us not to expect either of you to survive. He said that given your estimated weight of 745 grams, you had about a 20 percent chance of surviving. At an estimated 419 grams, Dr. Brown gave Jonas no chance.

All this time I'd worried about the lack of movement on your side, and now Jonas was given the lower odds. I knew now that the reason I hadn't felt you as much on my right side was because your distended sac had extended below Jonas's and you had apparently spent most of your time on my lower left side, where I thought you were Jonas. The reason you had initially been more active than Jonas was because the twin-to-twin transfusion syndrome (TTTS) had likely begun shortly after the twenty-week ultrasound.

We were still optimistic (either that or in denial or shock), despite Dr. Brown's grim odds. "You're still going to do everything you can to save them, aren't you?" I asked.

"Is that what you want?" Dr. Brown replied.

We both answered emphatically that we wanted you both to be given every possible chance. I don't know what prompted me to ask such a seemingly rhetorical question; but given his response, I'm glad we were able to make our wishes very clear. It helped us to have more closure afterwards when Jonas died.

The anesthesiologist arrived a little before 3:30 a.m. to

administer the epidural. Dr. Marshall had been a pediatri-
cian before switching to anesthesiology. While the other doctors emphasized the low odds, Dr. Marshall injected a bit of
optimism into the situation. He remembered a couple of
cases when things looked even worse than they did now for
Jonas, and the baby had survived. Although he stressed that
Jonas's survival (and yours too, for that matter) was
unlikely, it was at least *possible*.

I couldn't feel the contractions at all after the epidural.
Once again I was tempted to savor what might be the final
moments of my sons' lives by listening to your heartbeats on
the monitor. But this was the second night in a row that I
hadn't had any sleep, so once again I decided to rest and
conserve energy. Daddy agreed.

At the nurses' station was a monitor that traced your
vital signs. Daddy had been gazing intently at it through the
glass wall of my room, following your heartbeats on the
screen. Overcome with weariness, he dozed off and slept fit-
fully in a folded-flat hospital chair beside my bed.

I awoke two hours later at 5:30 a.m. I thought something
felt strange again, so my nurse summoned Dr. Metzgar. Dr.
Metzgar said I was now fully dilated and ready to deliver.

Chapter Six

The obstetrical team and the two neonatal teams began assembling in the C-section delivery room. I didn't need a C-section, but with two resuscitation teams required for you and Jonas, they needed the extra space.

We had barely adjusted to the idea of our tiny twins, and now you would probably both die. I was so upset about your imminent delivery that I vomited again. The nurse wheeled my bed to the delivery room as quickly as possible.

You were born at 6:13 a.m. and were promptly whisked away by the first NICU resuscitation team. The doctors were glad you were born first. The firstborn of preemie twins typically does better than the second. The doctors all felt it would have been a shame to waste the advantage of being firstborn on Jonas, who was expected to die anyway.

You were 11 inches long and weighed only 552 grams (1 pound, 3½ ounces) — much less than the predicted 745 grams. Your weight placed you in about the tenth percentile of babies born at this gestation. You'd been given only a 20 percent chance of survival based on your estimated weight of 745 grams. I wonder what odds they would have given you if they had known you would weigh almost 200 grams less.

Jonas was born two minutes after you, at 6:15 a.m., and was taken by the second team. He was also 11 inches long. He weighed 481 grams—slightly more than predicted but still small enough that his weight wasn't even listed on the growth chart. Jonas was well below the fifth percentile.

Daddy said that both you and Jonas looked blue and tiny, but otherwise incredibly normal.

You went to the warmer bed on the right, and Jonas went to the one on the left. Index cards were taped on the end of each bed. Your index card had a big capital "A" on it and Jonas's a big "B".

Dr. Brown was in charge of the team that worked on you, and Dr. Marshall headed the team that worked on Jonas.

Daddy prayed fervently, "Please, Lord, my little boys, please, Lord . . ." over and over and over, never doubting that you would both survive. I didn't pray at all. Part of me was in denial. I just couldn't comprehend the severity of the situation. Another part of me knew how bad it was; but I felt so sure God would fix everything that begging God to intervene could show a lack of faith. Despite the odds, we both had complete faith that you and Jonas would both live. It *had* to turn out fine. People were praying, after all.

Daddy saw Dr. Marshall shake his head as they worked over Jonas. Shortly afterwards, Dr. Brown came over and told us they had worked on Jonas for twelve minutes and had given him four doses of epinephrine — the maximum amount — to try to bring his heart rate up. Despite their efforts, Jonas's heart rate never rose above fifty beats per minute. It needed to stay above 100, at the minimum. Ideally, it should have been between 120 and 150. Essentially no oxygen was getting to his brain. They could do nothing more for him.

Although spoken softly, the words seemed to reverberate throughout the room, clanging in my head as I struggled to grasp the reality of what I had just heard. Jonas was *dead?* Our babies weren't supposed to die. I raised my anguished, tear-glazed eyes heavenward in an unspoken plea. *God, did this really happen?*

Daddy sobbed uncontrollably into my sleeve as a resident compassionately laid her hand on his back. The only words I can think of to describe Daddy's wailing are "raw grief." I have never heard anything like Daddy's weeping before or since, and I hope never to hear anything like it again.

They wrapped Jonas in a blanket and brought him to us. We had no idea how much time had gone by. Time was meaningless at that point. It wasn't until later, when we looked at Jonas's medical records, that we saw they discontinued CPR at 6:30 a.m. — at fifteen minutes of age. My medical record simply says, "Patient tolerated delivery well. Baby A to NICU. Baby B expired." It's strange how some of the most life-changing events can be reduced to a few scribbled lines on a medical chart.

Your medical records show that you had initially looked

as bad as Jonas. Your heart rate had started out in the forties, and you had also required four doses of epinephrine. You were ten minutes old when your heart began beating normally. It shocked us when we realized that you had been within minutes of dying also.

After they stabilized you, they wheeled you past my bed in a transport incubator on your way to the NICU. Daddy got a good look at you. Still numb from the epidural, I struggled to sit up enough to see you. Although I hardly saw you, I told them to go on anyway. I didn't want to delay your arrival in the NICU.

Soon they returned me to the glass-walled, high-risk OB room. We went from having about ten medical personnel in one room to just Daddy and Jonas and me. Daddy and I held Jonas's tiny, still body, looked at him, and cried. We thought about how Jonas would never cry, never nurse, never smile, never get a bath . . . never sleep in the bunk bed we'd purchased just last week. Every time we had our tears in check, the thought of that bunk bed brought another round of weeping. All our hopes and dreams for Jonas were shattered.

No one came into my room. Every time I heard footsteps, I cringed, thinking someone was coming to tell us that you had died too.

As I held Jonas I noticed that he would occasionally open his mouth, seeming to gasp for air. It reminded me of how a fish I caught in Grandpa's pond had opened and closed its mouth. At one point, I put my finger in Jonas's open palm, and he closed his hand around it. His hand was so small that it barely reached halfway around my index finger. I figured they were post-mortem reflexes.

We examined his tiny body. He was so perfect. Jonas had a narrower face than you because he had been squished up against my ribs, and he had a small scuff on the back of his head from the attempted resuscitation. Otherwise there was nothing whatsoever wrong with either of you. It wasn't like you boys had a birth defect or an inherited disease or anything. You were both perfect. The only defect lay in the shared placenta with the connecting blood vessels. And now Jonas was dead and your survival uncertain. Things had gone so wrong so fast.

Around 8:00 a.m. Dr. Rosato came to the door of my room. He told me he'd just been to the NICU, and that you were doing well. He said someone would come tell us something soon. I don't know how long he stood there at the door, just watching. I think he needed to know that we were coping okay with this tragedy.

I blew my nose and tossed the tissue into the trash can in the corner of my room.

"Nice shot," Dr. Rosato commented.

"I had a lot of practice when I was so big and couldn't get up," I answered.

Still in the doorway, he said, "You guys are strong. You'll get through this."

"I know we can be strong," I answered as I looked down at Jonas, "I just didn't want to have to be."

After another pause, Dr. Rosato said, "You seem to be holding up well."

"What are we going to do?" Daddy asked. "Quit?"

"Some people do." Dr. Rosato held Daddy's gaze for a moment as his answer sank in.

I asked Dr. Rosato at one point if he wanted to look at Jonas.

"I already saw him," he answered.

At my urging, he came forward to look at Jonas anyway.

"He looks like his mother," he said after barely a glance.

This gave me an interesting perspective on doctors. It was one thing for him to stand in my doorway and observe Daddy and me. It was quite another for him to look our dead baby in the face. I realized that this wasn't easy for him either. He'd just lost a patient. I suppose that's not something an obstetrician expects to happen. I'm sure he was used to miscarriages, but not a 24-week twin who'd looked so normal less than four weeks before.

Shortly after Dr. Rosato left, Dr. Brown came. I wondered if Dr. Rosato had sent him, telling him how anxious we were.

Dr. Brown said you were doing well — that you were hour-to-hour now instead of minute-to-minute. He estimated that you now had about a 25 percent chance of surviving. They would be doing an ultrasound of your head to detect any bleeding in the ventricles of the brain, a common problem in micro preemies.

Ventricles are small, fluid-filled spaces near the center of the brain. We all have two, one on the right and one on the left. Brain bleeds are classified from Grade I to Grade IV. Dr. Brown explained that Grade I and II bleeds fill some of the ventricle — not that serious in terms of your long-term outlook. Grades III and IV were another matter. A Grade III bleed fills the ventricle and pushes out on the surrounding brain tissue, expanding the size of the ventricle. A Grade IV bleed is a step beyond the Grade III. In addition to the enlarged ventricle of the Grade III, Grade IV bleeds continue, seeping into the surrounding brain tissue and destroying any brain tissue where the blood goes. If you had a Grade III or IV, you would be at tremendous risk for serious physical or mental disabilities. Dr. Brown painted a very grim picture for Grades III and IV, saying that some parents even choose to discontinue care of those babies.

I asked Dr. Brown if you and Jonas were identical. He said yes, explaining that TTTS *only* occurs in identicals and that you and Jonas looked alike to him anyway. He said that Jonas appeared not to have any defects but he could order an autopsy if we wanted. We declined. We knew what caused Jonas's death — extreme prematurity. It was more important to us to hold him than to get an autopsy. Besides, we couldn't stand the thought of someone slicing open his tiny body to examine the delicate little organs that God had knitted together inside me.

We asked if we could go see you in the NICU. Dr. Brown gently pointed out that Jonas's presence in the NICU would be inappropriate. We understood that, but what were we to do? We couldn't leave Jonas on my bed while we went to see you, and we were nowhere near ready for the finality of sending him to the morgue. Yet we really wanted to see you. Now that Jonas had died, I expected you to die too. I wanted to see you while you were still alive, so that I could treasure the memory in my heart.

Glancing at Jonas, Dr. Brown asked if we wanted him to call any clergy for us. Daddy and I laughed as Daddy said, "I *am* clergy." Dr. Brown looked surprised. With all the stubble on Daddy's face, he didn't fit the stereotypical image of a pastor.

Soon after Dr. Brown left, a nurse came and took Jonas for some pictures. As a courtesy to grieving parents, the hospital took a whole roll of pictures (12 shots) of any baby who had died, at no charge to the parents.

When the nurse returned Jonas to us, he was dressed in a small blue flannel gown and wrapped in a small quilt. The nurse also gave us some baby blankets, a small yellow rose, and a small stuffed dog for Jonas. I noticed that his hands

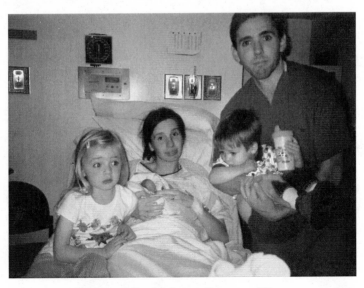

Patience, Wendy, Jonas, Owen, and Russ

49

were already getting stiff and cold—not at all like when he had held my finger.

Around midmorning, all four of your grandparents arrived with Patience and Owen. Patience took a turn holding Jonas while Owen played with the crank that raised and lowered my bed. The arrival of our parents solved the dilemma of what to do with Jonas while we went to see you. Your grandparents all took turns holding Jonas in my room while Daddy and I went down the hall to the NICU.

Chapter Seven

In the NICU, babies do not have separate, private rooms. It is a very large room with warmer beds, cribs, and incubators.

You weren't in a regular incubator like the other preemies, but in a "tent" of thick, clear plastic sheeting placed over your warmer bed. The humidity inside the tent kept your fragile skin moist. A special light shone down on you to help with newborn jaundice. To protect your eyes from the light, you wore a mask that made you look like a bandit.

Your whole body was very red—like a very bad sunburn. We could see your heartbeat through the thin skin over your rib cage. IV's went into your belly button, using your umbilical blood vessels. You had a breathing tube connected to a ventilator. We could follow your vital statistics in graph and number form on the monitor screen at your bedside.

Your nurse said you'd had a good blood gas. I had no idea what that meant, but I was glad it was good. We later learned it is a blood test that measures the oxygen, carbon dioxide, Ph level and other things in the blood so doctors can adjust the ventilator settings.

I never would have dared to ask, but the nurse said we could touch you. She explained that preemies at your level of development have very sensitive nerve endings, and that it would be extremely painful for you to be stroked, but we could gently touch you.

I lifted a flap of your tent and touched the sole of your foot. It seemed the least likely place to introduce potentially deadly germs to you. Daddy did likewise.

As bad as you looked, we thought you looked good. We didn't focus on the tubes and wires and the beeps of your equipment, or on the fact that our dead Jonas actually looked better than you at the time. We just saw our baby — our pathetically thin, little, displaced fetus whom we so desperately wanted to live.

Once we returned to my room, Daddy took your grandparents to see you too.

After we had all visited you and were settled back in my room, Dr. Brown reappeared and asked your grandparents to step outside so he could speak to Daddy and me privately. I knew it was going to be bad when he asked our parents to leave.

He told us that you had the dreaded Grade IV brain bleed on the left side of your brain, and a Grade I bleed on your right. He explained that although the blood would eventually be reabsorbed into the brain, the damage could not be undone. Any part of the brain where the bleeding had gone would remain damaged.

Not only did that practically guarantee a lifetime of handicaps — it also posed short-term risks, lowering your chances of survival to less than 20 percent. Often with a severe bleed like yours, the blood will form large clots as it reabsorbs into the brain. These clots sometimes lodge in the base of the brain where the spine begins, and block the flow of the cerebrospinal fluid. This results in water on the brain, causing increasing pressure inside the brain, which requires a shunt to keep the fluid from building up.

This was daunting information. Did we want to discontinue care? I asked Dr. Brown if we needed to decide right then, or if we could simply say to continue your care for now, but have the option to decide later to remove you from the life support. He had painted such a grim picture of the Grade IV, that I almost felt guilty for wanting to continue full intervention for you. Daddy never felt one bit guilty about continuing. He'd already lost one son that day, and he was not going to willingly hand another one over to the grave.

When Daddy told Dr. Brown we didn't want to discontinue care, Dr. Brown mentioned a friend's son had had a Grade IV. The boy was now thirteen and had just celebrated his first Communion. I think he meant the story to be an encouragement, but I was simply confused. How could a child with a Grade IV bleed take Communion? You mean he could chew the bread and swallow the juice? This was encouraging news, but why had we not been given the full spectrum of possibilities before making the life-or-death decision? Would Dr. Brown have shared that story if we had decided to remove your life support? I had pictured a future with you sitting expressionless in a wheelchair, unable to do anything for yourself. We didn't know which scenario to expect.

When we told our parents about the Grade IV, they said they'd support us no matter what we decided. I pled with God to simply let you live — regardless of potential disabilities.

Having our parents there was such a comfort. I noticed Grandpa struggling for composure. His eyes were wet behind his glasses and an occasional tear streaked down to his beard. He wanted to be strong for us, but I felt more strengthened by his tears — knowing that Jonas meant that much to him — than if his face had been firm and tearless.

Grandma had brought our camera and camcorder. Daddy took some videos of Patience holding Jonas and of Owen playing with my bed crank. Soon after that, our parents left and took Patience and Owen back home.

Around 11:30 a.m. Dr. Brown came into my room again. As he placed his stethoscope over Jonas's tiny chest he said to me, "I'm sorry, Mrs. Boyd, but the law requires me to listen for the absence of a heartbeat before I can sign the death certificate."

I had the presence of mind to ask, "Why didn't you do that before you handed Jonas to us in the delivery room?"

"Because he wasn't dead yet."

"Well, how long did it take him to die?"

"Probably an hour or two."

"After you handed him to us, Jonas was opening his mouth and gasping. Was he still alive then?" I could hardly choke out my questions.

Dr. Brown confirmed that Jonas had been alive when he was doing that and added, "He probably died in your arms."

I just nodded and didn't question any further. Neither Daddy nor I knew what to think. Between your condition and our questions about Jonas, we simply had too much to absorb. I wondered later if he died while the nurse was dressing him and taking his picture, or if he really did die in my arms. That question haunted me until we got the pictures the nurse had taken of Jonas. When I saw his stiff hands in the photographs, I knew he had already died before the nurse had taken him.

Just before lunchtime, the nurses moved me to another room. They'd promised to put me in the gynecology ward, so I wouldn't hear babies crying. But there were no other patients in the gynecology ward. They would have had to send a nurse out just for me, so I ended up in the maternity ward. They placed me in an out-of-the-way room at the end of a long hall. I only once heard a baby cry, and even then only very faintly. The nurses taped a picture of a yellow rose on my door as a symbol to medical personnel that we'd just lost a baby.

My brother Brad stopped by briefly. And my friend Kristin came to visit also. It must have been strange for her to see us holding Jonas, because she was pregnant and due just two weeks before I had been. Pastor Dean also came. I was holding Jonas when he entered my room.

"Do you want to see him?" I asked Pastor Dean.

"Oh, no," he hastily answered. "Germs, you know."

I realized he must have thought I was holding you, so I explained to him, "This isn't Hiram; this is Jonas."

Pastor Dean apologized profusely, and we assured him it was okay. Had you both lived, it probably would have been a common occurrence, but this was the only time that someone saw one of you and mistook him for the other.

Pastor Dean held Jonas for us while we went to visit you again in the NICU. When we returned, he thanked us for the opportunity and told us it had been a very touching experience for him. He then went to our apartment and picked up a bag of personal items I had asked Grandma to pack for me.

By far the most meaningful visit was from our friends Vaughan and Tammy Hayden. Vaughan, youth pastor at a church in Maryland, had graduated with Daddy just the week before. They had lost a set of twins at sixteen weeks, and their younger son had also been a twin. His twin had disappeared sometime in the first trimester. They cried with us; we felt so understood by them. We asked Vaughan to do Jonas's funeral service. He had never done a funeral before, but he agreed without hesitation.

Between visits I made phone calls to old friends and asked them to pray. I called everyone I could think of, even people I hadn't spoken to for years. You needed all the prayer you could get.

Finally, around suppertime, all our visitors had gone and the room was silent, leaving only Jonas and Daddy and me. Every time we thought we were ready to hand him over to the nurse, we balked and decided to keep him just a little longer. We knew these few hours would have to last a lifetime. Once we gave Jonas to the nurse, we would never in this life hold him again.

We did all the things for him we had done for our first two newborns—as much as we could in those few hours. We cuddled him, rocked him, looked at him, sang to him:

Oh, how He loves you and me,
Oh, how He loves you and me,
He gave His life, what more could He give?
Oh, how He loves you, oh how He loves me,
Oh, how He loves you and me.

Jesus to Calvary did go,
His love for Jonas to show,
What He did there brought hope from despair,
Oh, how He loves you, oh, how He loves me,
Oh, how He loves you and me.

We could barely get through the song for the tears welling up and our voices cracking.

Finally around 10:30 that night we were ready to let Jonas go. The nurse came with a stainless steel cart and some blankets. She laid Jonas on the blankets and put a blue hat on his head, saying she always hated to think of babies in the cold morgue with no hat. Then she tucked the blankets over him so that he was completely covered and wheeled him out.

Without question, giving Jonas to the nurse to be taken to the morgue is the hardest thing I have ever had to do. It's been over a year now as I write this, but I can barely see the page for the tears. Even now, a year later, I still yearn to claw my way back through time to hold him even one minute more.

I could hardly stand the thought of our tiny son, sixteen weeks younger than a typical newborn, lying cold and stiff in the morgue. You would expect to find much older people in the morgue — people who had lived full lives; but not our tiny Jonas. Even the word "morgue" sounded so gruesome — so dead.

This was not at all the way things were supposed to be. We'd been expecting two sweet, cuddly newborns. Now we had one stiff dead baby in the morgue and one very fragile baby in the NICU. The loss of sleep the previous two nights was now a blessing. Daddy and I fell easily into a deep and dreamless sleep. Even the occasional pop of one of my ribs snapping back into place did little to keep me awake.

Sunday, May 19, 2002

We awoke the next morning surprisingly refreshed. About 8:00 a.m., Dr. Rosato came into my room. "Don't ask yourself the 'what if' questions," was all he said.

After he left, Daddy and I puzzled over it, because we had just been discussing that very subject. We decided that some degree of "what ifs" was probably helpful just in dealing with our grief. Rather than shove aside the questions, we felt we should let ourselves ask them, be done with it, and then move on.

We visited you once more before I checked out of the hospital. You had been stable through the night. The nurse said that most preemies go home around their due date. It seemed pretty optimistic to discuss your homecoming, considering your uncertain condition. Sensing our incredulity, she told us that she had just sent home a twenty-four weeker a few days before.

"So you've had babies here who were as early as Hiram?" Daddy asked.

"Oh, yeah," she reassured us, "we've had ones this small before."

After praying over you, we returned to my room, gathered my things, and left for home.

Chapter Eight

It seemed strange and quiet with just Daddy and me in the car. I had gone to the hospital pregnant and now I was going home not pregnant, and with no babies. As Daddy drove, I was amazed by how unchanged the passing scenery was. Why, there was that same big stack of railroad ties! Hadn't they done *anything* to the tracks? Then I remembered that we'd been gone less than two days.

It seemed like a lifetime ago that we had left for the hospital on Friday. It *was* a lifetime—for Jonas. As traffic whizzed by, I marveled at how normal everyone else's lives still seemed to be.

We arrived home just before lunchtime. Grandpa came home from church soon afterward with some cookies and a big jug of chicken soup that Joy, an older lady at church, had made for us.

As I put the food away, I noticed the yellow flowers in the vase on the kitchen table— the buttercups Patience and Owen had picked for me only two days ago. I thought how uncertain life can be—just like the flowers of the field. The buttercups were still alive, and Jonas was dead.

Your Great-Grandma Fern (Grandma's mother) stopped by around noon. She dropped off a card and commented that she'd never seen cookies bigger than the ones Joy had made for us. Not a word about you, not a word about Jonas.

After Great-Grandma left, we looked at my parents incredulously and I asked, "Doesn't she know?"

She knew, of course. Even if she was uncomfortable with the subject of Jonas, I wished she had at least asked about you. If she was uncomfortable with it, how did she think Daddy and I felt? We opened the envelope, expecting a sympathy card. It was an anniversary card. We'd almost forgotten. Seven years tomorrow.

Daddy contacted Wilde's Funeral Home and agreed that we would meet with them that evening to make the arrangements. We wanted to get funeral plans out of the way today and still make some attempt at preserving tomorrow to celebrate our anniversary. Al Menger, one of Daddy's classmates from school, and his wife Pauline agreed to join us at the funeral home. Though they said little, their mere presence was a great comfort to us.

Bill Wilde discounted everything. I can't remember how many times he looked at the standard charge for a service and said, "I can't charge you that much for *that.*"

We bought their smallest casket—only 18 inches long. It was a vault and casket in one unit, made of cast concrete covered in velvet. Ironically, when Grandpa was a teen, he had a summer job building these little caskets, which they called "baby rests." When Grandpa told me about them, I never imagined that we would someday need to buy one.

The Wildes had been burying Boyds for generations, and they really sympathized with us. Bill Wilde personally made the hour-long drive to Reading to pick up Jonas's body, something he usually paid someone else to do. He also generously allowed us to defer payment until things "settled down" with you.

Daddy's parents offered us their burial lot for Jonas, and we gratefully accepted. We could bury Jonas three feet down on Pop Pop's side, and then exhume Jonas's casket and lay it aside temporarily for Pop Pop's burial someday.

When we got home, I made my first attempt at pumping breast milk. I didn't get much, but they had told me to save it anyway. I supposed it would be weeks before they gave you any. In fact, we were both still skeptical about your chances of survival. I felt foolish as I put the milk in the NICU freezer that night — for a baby who probably wouldn't live.

I still wonder if they didn't expect to dump the milk down the drain someday. That's what *I* expected. I'd been secretly praying that if you were going to die anyway, you would do it in time to make the funeral with Jonas so we wouldn't have to go through this twice.

Monday, May 20, 2002

Our seventh wedding anniversary. We decided to really treat ourselves and visit you *three times!* Grandma kept Patience and Owen while we went. Dr. Frederick Wirth was the neonatologist on service today.

As we approached your bedside, Dr. Wirth seemed surprised to learn that I was your mother. "You're looking good," he said.

I was saddened rather than flattered by his compliment. My flattening stomach only served to remind me that my babies were not where they belonged, and that the pregnancy and Jonas were being left farther and farther behind. You'd been born only two days before, and already it was hard to tell I'd even been pregnant. The dress I planned to wear to Jonas's funeral would fit just fine — the same one I had worn for Patience and Owen's baby dedications.

Even the little red spot on my wrist from my IV was fading. As long as that mark stayed, it didn't feel that long since I was in the hospital and still pregnant and Jonas still alive. That red mark made me still feel connected to Jonas.

We asked Dr. Wirth about your prognosis with the Grade IV brain bleed. He said it could cause anything from severe cerebral palsy and mental retardation to mild muscle weakness and coordination problems. Of course we latched our hopes to the mild end of the spectrum.

He also said you were amazing everyone with your progress. For the first time, I dared to ask what your chances now were. I expected that you might have climbed from your initial 20 percent chance of survival to 35 percent or so. We were elated when Dr. Wirth said 80 percent.

"Some would say that figure is optimistic," Dr. Wirth added, "but I *am* optimistic."

Eighty percent! This was the first really encouraging word we'd heard and was the best anniversary gift anyone could have given us.

We'd learned how to read the oxygen setting on your ventilator. The ventilator could be set anywhere from 21 percent oxygen, which equals the normal air we breathe, to 100 percent. The lower the oxygen setting, the better your lungs were working. We also learned how to read your oxygen saturation (or sats), a measure of the oxygen in your blood at any given time. They wanted your sats to be in the low- to mid-nineties. If your sats dipped below that, you were desaturating or "desatting." We were ecstatic to see your ventilator set to only 36 percent oxygen, yet your sats remained steady in the nineties, sometimes even climbing as high as ninety-eight.

We could also follow your heart rate and breathing on your monitor. It was mesmerizing to stare at the sine waves and heart rhythm waves dancing across the screen at your bedside. Sometimes we had to remind ourselves to look at you and not the monitor screen.

Later in our visit, your nurse showed us how to change your diaper and wet your mouth. Despite the high humidity in your little tent, your mouth easily became dry. The nurse dipped a cotton swab into a bottle of sterilized water and dabbed the inside of your mouth.

We couldn't believe how tiny your diapers were! They were a special micropreemie brand, and you wore size "fluff," the very smallest size. The diaper probably would have fit a typical plastic baby doll, but on you it came up to your armpits.

Between visits, we enjoyed a special anniversary meal

Grandma had prepared for us. Grandma took a picture of Daddy, Patience, Owen, and me as we cut our cheesecake. Somehow, by the grace of God, we managed to look normal, even cheerful, on the picture. You'd never know by our faces what had happened just two days before.

Tuesday, May 21, 2002

We began doing research about twins and TTTS. We wanted answers. Identical twins start out as one baby, and then split very early in the pregnancy. After our research, we could guess when you and Jonas had split. When an embryo splits before seven days, twins have separate sacs, separate placentas — separate everything, with no risk of TTTS.

If the split happens between seven and ten days, the twins will have separate amniotic sacs but share a placenta: the most common scenario. You and Jonas fit this description. You and Jonas no doubt could feel each other kick, but you never touched since you each had your own sac. Some of these twins (like you and Jonas) will develop TTTS. The earlier the TTTS starts in the pregnancy, the more difficult it is to manage.

If the split takes place at ten to fourteen days, the twins will not only share the placenta, but will also be in the same sac. Not only are these twins at risk for TTTS, but they also have a 50 percent chance of death from umbilical cord entanglement.

If the babies split after fourteen days, they will be conjoined.

The section in *Williams Obstetrics* about Dr. DeLia

especially intrigued me. Whereas other treatments only treated the symptoms of TTTS (like draining excess amniotic fluid), Dr. DeLia did a procedure that actually cured it. He used laser surgery to cut off the blood flow in the artery-to-vein connections in the placenta. The surgery is definitely risky and isn't a certain cure by any means, but we still wondered if it could have helped you and Jonas.

We were also trying to find people to donate blood for you. The previous summer, I'd read a book outlining some failures of the Red Cross to properly test its blood. But even more than AIDS- and hepatitis-tainted blood, we were concerned about some undiscovered disease. Many people contracted AIDS from blood transfusions in the early 1980s simply because no one knew the disease existed.

Your blood type is B positive. I'm AB positive, so I couldn't donate for you, nor would I have been allowed to so soon after delivery. We assumed that Daddy could, since he's O positive and anyone can get O. But the blood bank said any blood you received had to be B positive. Lorinda Dexter, a friend from the Mennonite school I'd graduated from, offered to put the word out at her church. We gratefully accepted her offer. We expected that Mennonite blood would be pretty safe, given their conservative lifestyle.

We still needed to choose a verse to be printed in Jonas's memorial cards and had countless other details to work out. We picked up extra copies of Tuesday's newspaper for Jonas's obituary. We had expected to do these things for our parents someday, but never for one of our children.

Pastor Dean was especially supportive. He even told us

not to worry about anything with Stone Hill Fellowship for the summer — to take the summer off and focus on you.

Chapter Nine

When I was a teenager, I had a feeling that God might someday take one of my children for the purpose of leading someone to Christ. In the years since I hadn't thought about it so much, but now it came back full force. I'd have a very hard time if someone, after years of exposure to the Gospel, became saved as a result of Jonas's death. I'd struggle with thinking, if they'd only believed sooner, Jonas wouldn't have needed to die. I wept before God.

And then it seemed as though God spoke to me: *My Son died so you could be saved.* That thought hit me like thunder. Who was I to withhold my son when He gave His? I felt chastened. But I also felt God's tender compassion. He understood my pain, for He had also lost a Son. Of all the people who had comforted us, God was one of the few who could truly say, "I know how you feel."

Yet still I questioned. *But it's different, Lord. Your Son came right back to You again, and now You're together forever in Heaven.* And again God answered, *And someday, you and your son will be together forever in Heaven too.*

Part Two

Silenced, I submitted to Him and to whatever He willed to happen.

When I shared this struggle with Pastor Dean earlier, he pointed out that God probably had many purposes to accomplish through Jonas's death. Someone's salvation could be just one piece to a very complex puzzle. And even if someone's salvation was the *only* purpose, I needed to be at peace with that. To my knowledge, no one was saved as a result of Jonas's funeral, even though Vaughan Hayden gave the gospel message loud and clear.

In the days following, I did an about-face in my thinking, hoping someone *would* be saved as a result of Jonas's death. His life seemed so short and his death so pointless. I wanted to see a reason for it—to see some good come out of it. I wanted to know *why* Jonas had died. But we often don't know why God allows things. That's a lesson I'm still learning. I have to be content to believe that someday we'll understand it all, even if I won't in this life.

When I was in the seventh grade an eighth grader died. Billy had had cancer on and off since he was ten years old. At one point, it looked as though he had licked the disease; but then it came back and killed him. He faced his death with a Christian grace and maturity beyond that of most adults, very much at peace. His parents and older sister were also very strong through it all. Many people were saved at his funeral. His parents saw God's kingdom furthered because of their son's death. I often craved that type of closure; but I know that even if God does not allow us to see the spiritual results of our tragedy, He still gives us the strength to carry on.

We needed that strength as we approached Jonas's funeral. It was a busy time as people called, visited, and brought or sent flowers and fruit baskets. Even Dr. Rosato called to see how I was doing. He said he'd been in to see you and you were amazing everyone with your progress. I was touched that he'd taken the time to check on you.

I was glad people cared, but grew weary of telling the story again and again. I felt as though Daddy and I were always on the phone, when we really needed to spend time with Patience and Owen and with each other.

And it seemed that every time we were finally ready to break away from things at home and go visit you, it was time for rounds or change of shift at the hospital. No parents are allowed in the NICU at these times, for privacy purposes — they don't want parents overhearing the medical staff discussing other people's babies.

We saw you only twice that day, but we got more good news. They planned to give you a little bit of breast milk through the feeding tube through your nose into your stomach. It made the pumping feel worthwhile. They would start with very small feeds — only 0.3 ccs (about 1/17 of a teaspoon) at first. They called this a trophic feed. It wasn't enough to really count as a feeding, and you still got all your nutrition through your IVs, but at least it would be a start.

My parents also visited. When Grandpa saw the other babies in the NICU and compared them to little 1¼-pound you, he called them "sumo-babies." I talked Grandpa into touching your foot once. That's the only time he touched you until you came home. Grandpa's an aerospace engineer, and in his analytical mind he figured the risk-to-benefit ratio weighed far too heavily against physical contact with you.

Wednesday, May 22, 2002

We took Patience and Owen to a lake in a state park for an hour. We often came to this lake and let Patience and Owen throw rocks into the creek that flowed out of it. Patience and Owen needed a normal day doing something familiar. They loved being there, and it was a nice break for us too.

Since you twins had been born, Patience and Owen had been somewhat out of control, and we hadn't been very consistent with discipline. They had been growing disobedient even before your birth, because I'd been physically unable to discipline them properly. And now all the stress and grief was affecting them. They also took advantage of our distraction with funeral arrangements and phone calls.

Once Patience and Owen were occupied, we got some much-needed peace. At home it seemed like the two of us had no time to talk. One subject we reluctantly discussed was a possible lawsuit. Might there be malpractice? Grandma and Grandpa insisted that Dr. Rosato had totally messed up, and that we needed to sue. We weren't ready to deal with the issue just yet. We could hardly even deal with the fact that Dr. Rosato may have made a fatal judgment in managing this pregnancy. I couldn't bear the thought that Jonas's death might have been prevented. But we still needed to discuss it. Did Dr. Rosato miss something? Did it cost Jonas his life? Would you be crippled because of it? Would you die?

Though we would never consider a lawsuit now, even then it was extremely distasteful to us. We'd grown close to our doctors and felt it would be like suing a friend. Yet a lot of people believed we were morally obligated to sue. They said we needed to keep Dr. Rosato responsible for his grave mistake and make him think twice before brushing off someone else's concerns.

We had only one dissenting opinion from someone we didn't even know. I'd asked Lorinda what she thought, and she in turn had asked a trusted friend of hers for advice. Her friend advised that we confront Dr. Rosato, taking an elder from our church with us. We discarded this advice since that's how the Bible says to confront a Christian brother. We didn't feel it applied when dealing with your doctor.

Although the idea of profiting financially from our son's death repulsed us, we resigned ourselves to eventually having to consider this more.

When we visited you that evening, we received even more good news. You had pulled out your breathing tube; and rather than put the breathing tube back in, they let you try something called CPAP (pronounced "see pap"). CPAP stands for "continual positive airway pressure." The CPAP had two prongs that fit snuggly into your nostrils and kept constant pressure going in so your airways and lungs would not collapse. The nurse could still adjust the percentage of oxygen, but you were breathing entirely on your own.

We couldn't believe the astounding progress you were making. Long-term ventilator use is very damaging to the lungs and often results in chronic lung disease. Even if you weren't able to remain on the CPAP for long, every day you spent breathing on your own meant that much less damage inflicted on your lungs by the ventilator.

One drawback of the CPAP was that some of the air went into your stomach. Because of this, they used something to gently suction the air out of your stomach. This meant stopping the trophic feeds. There was no sense in putting milk in your stomach just to have it sucked right back out. You had only received one trophic feed before you went on the CPAP. At that point, the doctors felt it was more important for you to be off the ventilator to minimize lung damage than for you to get such small feeds.

Chapter Ten

We were supposed to be at Wilde's funeral home by nine the next morning, a full hour before the viewing was scheduled to begin. We really wanted to visit you first, so we asked the nurses if they could waive their rule of no parents in the NICU during shift change from 7 to 7:30. Though sympathetic, they could not bend the rules; so we decided to visit you before change of shift.

Knowing we had to get up early and that we might have trouble falling asleep after such a stressful week, Daddy and I did something we'd never done before and have never done since. We each took two Benadryl to help us fall asleep.

Thursday, May 23, 2002

We stopped by the NICU at 6:45 a.m. and visited with you fifteen minutes before shift change. We were at Wilde's well before nine and spent time alone with Jonas before others arrived for the viewing. He looked so different than he had on Saturday. His little mouth turned down into a frown. I took his knit hat off to see if I liked him better that way and saw a big crease on the top of his head—probably his soft spot. The hat went back on. His hands were folded on top of his blanket, but his fingers looked so claw-like that I asked Daddy to tuck them back under his blanket. He didn't look like my little Jonas at all. I didn't want to remember him this way. I knew I'd better get my fill of looking on this final day, but I didn't look in such a way as to make an indelible memory in my mind. I focused on his nose, his blankets—things that still looked the same.

Daddy and I stood by Jonas's casket as people came for the viewing. We had a box of tissues on a small table behind us, and a trash can behind the table. We knew that some people, whether sincere or not, might say some insensitive things. I half expected someone to say that if we had stopped at two children, like most families, none of this would have happened. To avoid feeling hurt by such comments, Daddy and I decided to have a "most insensitive comment contest." At the end of the day, we'd compare notes, see who had said the most insensitive thing, and then laugh about it.

Although I cried, I felt mostly detached during the viewing, watching with interest people's expressions as they saw Jonas. Your Great-Grandma Fern clutched her chest and dissolved into tears. She was sufficiently grieved that I forgave her for Sunday. I truly think she just had not known what to say.

Great Mom Mom (Grandpa's mother) reacted much the same way. She clutched her chest with one hand, held her hankie to her face with the other, and leaned against Great Pop Pop for support. Even Great Pop Pop, a WWII-Marine veteran, had tears in his eyes.

A large crowd turned out for the funeral. We had made it clear that the funeral was not private; rather, we craved support. We also let it be known that parents were welcome to bring their small children or babies. If Jonas had been our only child, or if you had also died, seeing and hearing babies at the funeral might have bothered me. But since we still had Patience and Owen, and you seemed to be doing well, we didn't feel that we'd be bothered by the presence of little ones.

My friends Kristin, Lynne, and Denise came. They seemed truly heartbroken. All three were in tears. Denise and Kristin were both patients of Dr. Rosato and due within weeks of when I had been due.

Most of my Mennonite high-school friends came as well. I was the most surprised and touched to see Penny, Becky, and Curt from the self-storage where I had worked. They had closed the office to come. Penny had put signs on the office doors saying there had been a death in the family.

Vaughan Hayden's message was very meaningful, and the plan of salvation was very clear. We hoped for responses. We wanted to see some purpose for Jonas's too-short life and some good from his death. After Vaughan's message, we listened to a song Grandpa had written for Jonas.

"Jonas didn't have much in this world, just a blanket," Grandpa said, his voice breaking, "so I'm giving him this song."

I'd been holding my tears back, but it was such a sweet,

simple melody that my tears now streamed down.

Too soon, the service was over and everyone filed past the tiny casket for one last look at Jonas. Then it was our turn. Bill Wilde said we could take as long as we needed. We didn't rush, but we didn't linger either. We looked at Jonas, with Patience and Owen by our sides; then we sent them out, and we looked at him by ourselves.

I touched Jonas once, briefly. His skin had a cold unnatural feel to it. I'd known he would feel that way. I hadn't really wanted to touch him, but other people had touched him at the viewing, and I wanted Daddy's and my hands to be the last that touched him in this world.

Daddy had always wrapped up Patience and Owen a certain way when they were babies, and when we were done looking, Daddy wrapped the blankets around Jonas. When Daddy finished, Jonas was completely covered.

The weather was clear, breezy, and cool for the season. Under other circumstances, it would have been a beautiful day; but today the deep blue, cloudless sky and the windswept hilltop where we stood to bury Jonas just seemed bleak.

Pastor Dean did the graveside service. He charged everyone to stand by us for the whole next year, saying it would be the hardest. At the end of the service he invited everyone to a lunch at Mom Mom and Pop Pop's church just down the hill.

While Pop Pop led everyone to the church, Daddy and I stayed behind to watch them lower Jonas's tiny casket.

Whoever dug the hole had not squared off the corners enough, and the casket caught partway down. So they brought it back up and chipped the corners out a little more with a shovel. The casket still caught. After three or four attempts, they finally got it down the full three-foot depth — but crooked. Jonas's head is pointed slightly to the right and his feet to the left. We didn't know whether to laugh or cry.

The day you were both born and Jonas died was the most grief-filled day of my life; nothing else even comes close. But this was easily the most *difficult* day. I kept thinking, "That's my baby they're putting in the ground. That's my baby they're putting in the ground . . ."

They asked if we wanted to stay while they put the dirt back in. Daddy said no. I wanted to stay, but I didn't know if they were serious about their offer. Besides, I'd never known anyone to stay for that, and I thought it might look odd, so we walked away and got into the van. Daddy didn't start it up right away, so I turned in my seat and watched them shovel dirt back into the hole. Through my open window I could hear the scraping of the shovel against the dirt and stones. Each shovelful was like a physical beating to my heart. I kept thinking, "They're putting the dirt on my baby. They're putting the dirt on my baby . . ."

Once Daddy started the van, we went only about 200 feet before I asked him to pull off to the wooded edge of the cemetery. I couldn't control the tears anymore. That was the closest I'd come yet to totally letting myself go. After about ten or fifteen minutes of weeping, I felt ready to face everyone at the church.

When we arrived, I was surprised that I was actually hungry. We filled our plates and sat with family friends.

Later, I couldn't face people anymore, and I left the room and wandered through the church. Upstairs, I discovered a private, nicely decorated restroom just off the church balcony. It even had a box of tissues. I sat on the floor to cry. I must have been there at least an hour. I couldn't stop crying. I didn't really want to stop crying. My son had just been buried—I needed to cry. Daddy found me there later and sat with me for a while.

When I came down, most of the people had left. Around 3:00 p.m. we left also—or tried to. Earlier, on the way to the cemetery with our headlights on, Daddy had noticed the voltage drop. He had known the alternator was weak, but hadn't had time to replace it. The headlights had drained the battery on the way to the cemetery. We got a jump-start and headed home.

After spending some time with Patience and Owen, we went to the NICU and visited you. We were wrung out from the funeral; but we knew we needed to lay aside our grieving for Jonas and focus on the positive strides you were making.

We were both finally letting our guard down and allowing ourselves to believe that you would make it—especially now that the funeral was over. We just knew God would not make us go through a second funeral. Our previous worry over your survival was gone. We began talking about "when" you came home, not "if."

A nurse gave us the paperwork for your and Jonas's birth certificates. The staff hadn't realized that the paperwork had never been filled out. It seemed ironic — Jonas had a death certificate almost a week before his birth certificate.

When we finally felt tired enough to try going to sleep, we went to bed. Under our pillows we tucked the cordless phone and our cell phones as we had done every night since the previous Sunday. We tossed and turned and were just drifting off when the phone under Daddy's pillow rang.

Chapter Eleven

Daddy knew who it was even before he saw "Reading Hosp" on the caller ID. Who else would call at 11:45 at night?

It was Dr. Hoffman, one of the neonatologists. When I heard the shaky tone of Daddy's voice, I knew something terrible was happening to you.

"What are our options?" Daddy asked.

"We usually send them to Children's Hospital in Philadelphia." Dr. Hoffman responded.

"Are there any *other* options?" Daddy hates driving in Philadelphia.

"We could call Hershey and see if they have any beds open."

"Let's *do* that," Daddy replied.

Hershey Medical Center has an excellent reputation in our area. If someone needs a regional hospital, they go to Hershey.

Dr. Hoffman told Daddy we needed to sign a release form for you to be transferred. I whispered, "Tell him we can be there, like, *now!*"

When Daddy hung up, I asked the dreaded question, "What is it?"

Daddy said your bowel had perforated, and you needed surgery. Since Reading had no pediatric surgeons, they needed to fly you to Hershey.

"How bad is it?" I asked, mentally begging him to tell me everything would be okay.

"It's *bad*," Daddy said in a serious, urgent voice.

We called Grandma and she was instantly downstairs to watch Patience and Owen so we could leave. We were literally pulling on our clothes as we went out the door. The only things we brought with us were our cell phones and the breast pump.

We were both shaking uncontrollably. The last thing Grandma heard us say as we left was Daddy's whispered prayer, "Oh, God, please not the other one."

The battery in our 1988 Plymouth Reliant station wagon was weak, but we took it anyway because of the dead alternator in the van.

As Daddy drove, I phoned the NICU to ask if they could arrange for us to bypass the usual security hoops that late-night visitors have to jump through. They said they'd phone security and let them know we were coming. We had no idea how quickly your condition could deteriorate, and we wanted to get to your bedside as quickly as possible. We truly feared that you might be dead before we arrived. We parked in the first open stall in the parking garage and ran across the driveway to the hospital entrance.

As we rushed through the door, I breathlessly tried to explain our situation to the guard. The guard was a *big* man; he immediately got up and lumbered toward the door. I'll never forget his deadpan drawl: "I got the key; I'm openin' the door."

He handed us our visitors' passes as we ran through the door. We sprinted down the hallways and willed the elevator to go faster. We were at your bedside within twenty minutes after Daddy got off the phone with Dr. Hoffman.

Friday, May 24, 2002
12:15 a.m.

Dr. Hoffman didn't seem like a people person—more of an academic. He did ask us who was caring for our other children. Maybe he was concerned that, in our haste, we'd left them home alone.

Dr. Hoffman showed us the spot on one of your X-rays that had looked suspicious to him. Even when he pointed right to it, we couldn't tell anything. It wasn't even an X-ray of your bowels; it was a *chest* X-ray that just happened to show some of your bowel. Based on his suspicions, Dr. Hoffman had ordered an X-ray with you on your side. This second X-ray confirmed Dr. Hoffman's suspicion that there was air in your abdominal cavity. That's when he had called us.

He explained that your bowel was leaking waste and gas into your abdominal cavity, which would cause infection and death if left untreated. Dr. Hoffman had already started you on powerful antibiotics to try to keep the infection under control, but the surgery to repair your bowel would have to be done at Hershey.

Dr. Hoffman asked again if we wanted to discontinue care, and again we said no. We asked if they'd operate immediately or just observe you when you got to Hershey, and Dr. Hoffman said he wasn't sure. Because you were so small, he didn't know if you could even tolerate a major surgery. Maybe nothing could be done for you.

Your chances of survival had just majorly plummeted — just when we'd begun to allow ourselves to believe you would live. We'd just buried Jonas. We prayed earnestly. Unlike my denial in the delivery room six days before, I knew this was bad. Burying your brother just hours before was a reality check that this whole thing was serious.

Once again, we had to be strong, not only in losing Jonas, but also in dealing with the uncertainty of your condition. We knew that Jonas was in Heaven with Jesus, yet it caused us such mixed feelings. How could we thank God that Jonas was in Heaven and then pray so hard that you wouldn't join him? We tried to be thankful that Jonas wasn't suffering; yet you suffered every day as we tried to keep you here with us. After going around in our minds like that a few times, we couldn't think about it anymore.

I hated the emotional trauma of the uncertainty. I wished we could simply fast forward to the end of the summer and have you either home or dead. We knew there would be many ups and downs on the "NICU roller coaster" and I didn't know if we could handle it.

Just as she had done six nights ago, Grandma called people, waking them out of their slumber to pray.

Meanwhile, Dr. Hoffman left the NICU to sleep in the doctors' sleeping room. He gave strict instructions to the nurses not to wake him up for anything else regarding you unless absolutely necessary. Being the only neonatologist there that night, he probably needed to conserve energy to deal with any other potential crises that might arise with the other babies.

A hospital never sleeps, but it was nevertheless very still and quiet in the NICU at this time of night. The dimmed lights only made the waiting more awful. Sometimes I thought I could hear the clock ticking on the wall.

The nurses told us that the Hershey NICU transport team had to pick up a baby in Huntingdon before coming to get you. We went from being worried that we might hold things up by not getting to the hospital quickly enough, to wondering how long it would be until the helicopter would come. We alternated between watching your monitor and watching the second-hand on the clock slowly tick off time.

The nurses knew we were anxious and tried to estimate when the transport team would arrive. Maybe a forty-minute flight from Hershey to Huntingdon and then forty minutes back and then fifteen minutes to Reading.

Shortly before 3:00 a.m., someone from Hershey phoned to report that the transport team was leaving for Reading. Now Daddy and I really watched the clock. As anxious as we were to see you transported to Hershey, part of me wanted to hold on to these last minutes at Reading. Once you were at Hershey, you would be in a whole new world, faced with possible surgery and who knew what else. Although you had been here less than a week, we had become attached to this place.

I asked your nurse, Patty Bressler, "When a baby goes to Hershey, do they ever come back here again?"

"Occasionally," she answered. "We've had some come back."

I knew Hershey was a much larger hospital than Reading, and I expected it to be very impersonal as well. I wanted to know if we could hold onto the hope of coming back here again if you lived that long.

Patty seemed rather red-eyed, but her voice sounded normal as she said, "Hiram's very special to me. You don't remember me, do you?"

We looked up, puzzled, and shook our heads.

"I was the nurse who helped resuscitate Hiram," she said.

Here was one of the people who had helped save your life. Patty had seen you born and admitted to this NICU, and she was here now to see you leave for Hershey. I'm glad she told us who she was. I would never have recognized her.

We prayed over you and sang to you, making the most of our time. I kept glancing at the clock, wishing both to hold back time and to speed it up.

3:00 a.m. Another song. More prayers.

3:10 a.m. We sang the same song we'd sung for our Jonas. *Oh, how He loves you. Oh, how He loves me . . .* My voice cracked as I wondered if you were destined to the same fate as Jonas.

3:20 a.m. Was that a helicopter we heard? We'd been straining to hear for the last ten minutes, even as we sang and prayed, knowing the transport team could arrive any moment. As the next minute went by, we all heard Life Lion coming for you. At around 3:30, the transport team entered the NICU, accompanied by the same security guard who'd given us our visitors' passes over three hours before.

The transport team was made up of four people: the pilot, the flight nurse, a NICU nurse, and a respiratory therapist. After the paperwork was done, they began their efficient process of transferring you to their transport isolette. It was all too much for me. As much as I tried to maintain control, tears blurred my vision as I watched.

Through my tears, I kept a sharp eye out to make sure that nothing of yours was left behind or thrown out. I wished I had the letter "B" that had been taped to Jonas's warmer bed in the delivery room. We had so little that was his. I wasn't going to let any of your special things disappear.

Patty must have sensed how important such mementos were to us, because she handed a transport team member your hospital bracelet and said emphatically, "Don't lose this. If Hiram ever comes back to Reading, you give this to his mother, because they'll need it."

Daddy joked nervously, "I don't know—do you think the helicopter can handle that much weight?"

We signed the last of the papers and were instructed to

enter the hospital at Hershey through the emergency entrance. You would be in bed twenty-three in the Hershey NICU. We stayed in the Reading NICU until they wheeled you out. Then, after one last admonition from the Reading nurses *not* to speed, we left.

We were in such a daze, and the hospital looked so different with all the doors in the hallways closed at night, that we took a wrong turn and were temporarily lost. The delay was good, though, because we arrived outside just in time to hear the helicopter take off from the hospital roof.

"Come on!" I said as I grabbed Daddy's hand, "let's watch it!"

We ran out from under the covered walkway. The helicopter loomed large above us, hovering over the rooftop, its landing lights piercing down through the foggy, early-morning darkness. The sound of the shrieking rotors intensified, echoing between the hospital and the parking garage. Then it banked out over us, gained speed, and screamed away, disappearing beyond the parking garage.

Our tiny son was in that helicopter, being rushed away to a hospital we'd never seen. I broke down, sobbing uncontrollably.

When we got into our car, it wouldn't start. *Not again*, I thought — first the van at the funeral, and now the station wagon. The engine wouldn't even turn over. In our hurry to get inside three hours earlier, Daddy had accidentally turned the ignition switch back to "accessory." The already-weak battery was dead. A security guard loaned us a portable jumper, and soon we were headed toward Hershey.

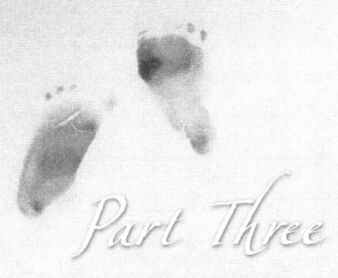

Part Three

Now faith is the substance of things hoped for,
the evidence of things not seen.
For by it the elders obtained a good report.

These all died in faith, not having received the promises,
but having seen them afar off . . .

Hebrews 11:1, 2, 13

Chapter Twelve

At about 4:30 a.m., we entered the parking lot at the Hershey Medical Center. The place had a modern-looking, black granite and glass entrance in contrast to Reading Hospital's Depression-era brick. Despite the farm-country setting, it looked huge and intimidating.

We entered the emergency waiting area as instructed. But no one was there—not in the waiting area, and not at the desk. After several long minutes, someone emerged from the depths of the reception area to help us. After we explained why we were there, the woman paged a chaplain to lead us to the NICU.

Then we waited for what seemed like a very long time, wondering when the chaplain would arrive. We sat on chairs near the main hallway so he would notice us as soon as he came.

The chaplain finally showed up a little after 5:00 and led us through a maze of hallways, pointing out the cafeteria along the way. We rode the elevator to the seventh floor and walked more hallways. Even in the dim, early-morning light, I could see the cheery décor of the pediatric floor of the hospital — not at all like the institutional "décor" at Reading. This place was almost *too* cheery, too modern, too big and impersonal. I didn't like it. I wished we could go back to Reading.

In one of the hallways, we heard a little boy plaintively calling over and over and over for his mommy. That was heartrending.

When we arrived at the NICU, we scrubbed and went in to see you. You lay on your back on an open warmer bed, like a small table with a thin mattress and blankets. It had very shallow clear plastic sides. A warmer light shone down on you.

Bed 23 was actually its own glass-enclosed room in one corner of the NICU. There were no walls as such — just solid pieces of glass with glass doors so the medical personnel could keep an eye on things from the main NICU.

After a brief visit with you, we stepped out to the main NICU to meet Dr. Charles Palmer, the neonatologist on call. He spoke with an accent, and later we learned he was South African. His explanations were very matter-of-fact and thorough.

He halfheartedly asked if we wanted to discontinue care for you. We could tell he asked the question only because their policy demanded it. We confirmed that we wanted to continue your care, and he simply moved on to discuss the situation at hand. We were never asked that question again.

Though we were surrounded by other babies and an occasional nurse, we hardly noticed them. All the lights were on in your room behind us, contrasting with the dim NICU. The X-ray viewer illuminated Dr. Palmer's face. As Daddy and I looked at the X-rays and focused on Dr. Palmer's words, it seemed that the only people in the world were you, Dr. Palmer, Daddy, and me.

Dr. Palmer explained that your bowels had NEC, a condition in which the bowels might be weakened or dead in places because of a lack of blood flow to your organs when you were being resuscitated just after your birth.

We asked if anything would be done immediately or if they'd just watch and wait. I explained that Dr. Hoffman had thought Hershey might simply observe you for a period of time. Dr. Palmer leveled a direct gaze at me and said emphatically, "That's not the way we do things here."

Good, I thought, *these people are proactive. They'll stay on top of things. They won't give up on Hiram.*

Dr. Palmer then moved to the subject of your brain bleed. We were surprised when he said that the affected area of your brain was likely to impact only your motor skills and not your intellect. One of my high school friends, Danita Good, had a twin who died. Danita and Darla had had twin-to-twin transfusion just like you and Jonas. Danita has cerebral palsy. Her right hand doesn't work at all and she limps, but there is little she cannot do. And she certainly always seemed up-to-speed intellectually. *Maybe he can be like Danita,* I thought. I felt that we could handle any physical limitations as long as your mind was intact.

Dr. Palmer explained that although the brain bleed should not affect your mental capacity, your prematurity could increase the likelihood of learning disabilities. He stressed the influence of your home life on your eventual outcome. I almost mentioned that we were planning on homeschooling anyway, but I kept quiet, thinking that might not impress him.

Next the surgical residents discussed their plan with us. Since you were far too small to tolerate a major surgery, they planned to insert a Penrose drain into your abdomen to wick out the stuff leaking from your bowels. They hoped that this, combined with antibiotics, would keep you alive until you were big enough for more extensive surgery. It was even possible, they said, that your bowel could heal itself, eliminating the need for additional surgery.

We signed the consent forms for the surgery and stayed by your bed until they were ready to begin. Dr. Cilley, the pediatric surgeon, reassured us that this was a fairly simple procedure. Everything about him, from his appearance and his diction, to the way he related to us, inspired confidence. He pointed the way to a room just outside the NICU where we could sleep while they operated.

In the room, we folded out the sofa bed, grabbed a few blankets from the shelf, and crashed. No more than an hour later, we heard a soft knock at the door. We were both instantly awake as Dr. Cilley came in.

"The surgery went well. It was a non-event, just as we expected," he said in his calm, confident way. "He'll probably look a little worse to you over the next three days or so as his body begins to react to infection. Now go back to sleep."

When we woke again, we looked out our window and marveled at the size of the place. From our vantage point on the backside of the seventh floor, there seemed to be countless wings, rising from the ground like a mountain range. Although the front entrance had a modern facade, everything else seemed to be constructed of sixties-era, water-stained concrete.

We called Grandma and Grandpa to update them so they could call everyone else, and then we went in to visit you sometime after 7:00 a.m. When your nurse changed your diaper, we saw your drain. You had two small incisions—one on either side of your belly. A small plastic tube went into one incision, through your belly, and out through the other incision. A safety pin through each end of the tube held it in place. The nurses fit pieces of gauze around the ends of the drain to collect the gunk the drain wicked out. They weighed and replaced the pieces of gauze every few hours so they could track the amount of drainage. After this surgery, we could always tell your X-rays by the bright white safety pins.

When we went to the cafeteria for breakfast, we were surprised to see a classmate of Daddy's, Rob Ail. I'd almost forgotten that he was a nurse at Hershey. He spent his entire break listening to us and praying with us. It was uplifting to have Rob pray with us, and to know that for about forty hours a week, he was somewhere at this hospital.

After breakfast, we returned to the NICU to find Deb Smeltz (another of Daddy's classmates who worked at Hershey), and her teenage son waiting for us. They had also

heard that you'd been transferred to Hershey. The Lord used
Deb and Rob to give us two big doses of encouragement
right when we needed it.

After Deb's visit, we fell asleep in our chairs at your bedside. We woke when Dr. Cilley entered. He gave us more
details about your condition, reminding us that you would
probably be at your worst for the first three days or so after
surgery. He also said that although preemies often have an
initial "honeymoon period" with their lungs, the lungs typically decline and are at their worst between seven and ten
days after birth. If a baby gets through the tenth day, things
often begin to improve. You would be seven days old the
next day. The combination of your declining lungs and your
post-operative status concerned us.

Grandma and Grandpa came to see you later that morning while a family friend kept Patience and Owen at home.
Grandma and Grandpa talked and cried with us in the parents' rooming-in room and then treated us to lunch in the
cafeteria.

Grandma and Grandpa had brought our camera and
camcorder. We wanted to capture you on film while you
were still alive so we wouldn't end up with nothing but
dead-baby pictures like we had of Jonas. We took video of
your whole body, then of your face and hands and feet. Your
arms were out at your sides, palms up. Your legs were
slightly drawn up, knees bent out to the sides, the soles of
your feet facing each other. We could hear the hiss of your
ventilator and see the mechanical rise and fall of your chest
as the machine breathed for you. I slid my finger under your

hand and then under your foot to give some scale of size in the video. Your tiny fingers barely reached across my thumbnail. You were so small that the camera couldn't even focus as Daddy zoomed in on your hand and your foot.

"You've got a lot of people praying for you, little guy," Daddy said softly as he prepared to shut off the camcorder.

A hospital social worker told us about the Ronald McDonald House, where non-local parents of hospitalized children could stay free of charge. Since it was full that night, we stayed with some friends of my parents who lived nearby.

Saturday, May 25, 2002

The next morning we met Dr. Eric Michael, who would be your neonatologist for the next week and a half. He seemed very compassionate and understanding of all we'd gone through; he reminded me a lot of Dr. Brown.

Dr. Michael reminded us that although you looked stable, you were entering some potentially rough days because of your post-operative status and your lungs. We really wanted to go home for Patience and Owen, but didn't want to leave you at this critical time.

"The surgeons said Hiram's bowel might heal itself," we said. "How likely is that?"

"About forty percent of the time in cases like Hiram's, the bowel will heal itself," he answered. "In fact, we had a baby here once who actually grew a new section of bowel."

I wondered if that had been a miracle, or if there had

been some medical explanation. I would have felt better if it were the latter. After losing Jonas, I had more confidence in the doctors' *ability* than in God's *willingness* to heal you.

I knew God could work and somehow be glorified through Jonas's death. I tried to convince God that He didn't need another death — that He could be glorified by your disability instead. I didn't even pray for complete health with no disabilities. At this point we just wanted you to live, no matter what your condition. We wanted to take our little Hiram home with us at the end of the summer.

We asked Dr. Michael if we could donate blood for you. He gave us the phone number for Hershey's blood bank and promised to try to hold off transfusing you until we had some directed blood available for you. You needed transfusions regularly because you were too small to replace the volume of blood routinely taken for lab tests. A vial of blood is nothing to an adult or even a child; but for preemies, it's a significant portion of the total blood volume.

You had already received a few transfusions at Reading, and we had just completed the paperwork for directed donations there. A Mennonite lady that Lorinda had talked to was B positive and was willing to donate, but you were transferred before she had the chance. Now that we were dealing with a different blood bank, we had to start over.

Later in the day, you were moved out to the main NICU. They needed bed twenty-three for another baby. You no longer lay in the open warmer bed, but in an isolette with a fitted blanket covering it to keep it as dark and womb-like as possible.

Your bed was between a girl named Kyra and a boy
named Caleb, both in covered incubators like yours. We
learned later that Kyra had been due one day before you and
born two days before you. We saw Kyra a few times when
her parents lifted up the blanket on her isolette. As I
watched her mother chat easily with the nurses, I wished I
felt as comfortable here.

We never saw Caleb. We learned that Caleb was a twin.
His brother was at the other end of the NICU. Caleb died
about two weeks later.

Mom Mom and Pop Pop had spent a few hours at our
apartment earlier that day to give Grandma and Grandpa a
break from Patience and Owen. Pop Pop had also bought
and installed an alternator for our van and bought a new
battery for our station wagon. Mom Mom and Pop Pop came
to visit us at Hershey later in the day. This was the first
they'd seen you since the day you were born.

That night the Ronald McDonald House had a room for
us. When we arrived, a kind woman named Michelle Jayne
checked us in. We told her our story as briefly as possible.

"You probably hear stuff like this all the time," I told
her.

"Actually, not that often," she replied.

She said most people stayed here for only a few days
while their children had surgery or went to Hershey's
world-renowned feeding clinic.

Michelle gave us our keys and then gave us a tour of the

house, explaining how things operated. The upstairs was like a hotel. Each family had its own private room and bathroom, which we were expected to keep clean. Downstairs were a communal kitchen, living room, dining area, family room, playroom, and laundry facilities.

Michelle showed us the pantry area where each family had its own small cabinet for food storage. Several cabinets had "House food," for any House guests to help themselves. In the big commercial refrigerator and freezer, each family had a private bin, in addition to House bins that anyone could take from.

"Help yourselves to whatever food you want," Michelle encouraged us. "Don't ever feel like you're taking the last of something. There's always plenty more stored in the basement."

Michelle was so welcoming. Living in a house that wasn't ours and helping ourselves to food that wasn't ours went against our grain. But Michelle made us feel at home. Our stay at the Ronald McDonald House (RMH) was made much easier because of the first impression Michelle gave us.

At the House, we met a young couple named Chris and Sarah Caldwell whose youngest daughter had just been discharged from the NICU. She had weighed two pounds and something at birth. Chris tried to encourage us, saying, "They do a lot of good things here at Hershey."

He seemed confident that you would do well in the capable hands of the NICU staff. But whenever someone tried to encourage us with their own NICU story, I asked what their baby had weighed. If it was over two pounds, I just tuned them out, politely listening on the outside, but ignoring them inside, thinking, *What do you know? Was your baby this tiny? Did your baby need surgery?*

Chapter Thirteen

Not all the cases here at Hershey were simple. Some were every bit as serious as yours. As Daddy and I rode the elevator to the seventh floor, we struck up a conversation with a woman who was also going to the children's hospital. She was from Florida, visiting her four-month-old granddaughter Abigail. Abigail and her sister Bronte had had TTTS. Bronte was out of the hospital, but Abigail was on her fourth bowel surgery. Abigail's grandmother said that her liver, kidneys—everything—looked bad.

"I don't think she's going to make it," she confided.

I listened in amazement. I never expected to meet someone else who'd dealt with TTTS. I briefly shared our story, and we parted ways, promising to pray for each other's babies.

A week or so later when I mentioned Abigail to Todd Layser, the RMH house manager, he told me Abigail had pulled through that bad episode.

"Yeah," Todd said, "there've been lots of times that she's looked like she wasn't going to make it, but she keeps pulling through." He motioned to the wall where a newspaper article about Abigail was posted. The article must have been written back in her more stable days, because it definitely implied that they expected Abigail to survive.

I heard a couple of weeks later that Abigail died at the age of five months. The next time I looked at the wall in the RMH office, the article was gone.

During our early days at Hershey we were really open and friendly with people who wanted to talk. And there were *lots* of them. But after a while, I grew weary, even a little paranoid, of people and their sad stories — especially accounts that didn't seem like a big deal to me. I was tired of hearing about people whose children were in for surgery and would be back home in a week.

Sometimes I would feverishly push the "door close" button on the elevator before anyone else could come around the corner wanting to board. I needed that little bit of solitude, because anyone whose child was new to the hospital (which was most people) was too wrapped up in his own situation to hear anyone else's story. It was even worse when I saw fellow NICU parents and heard about twins who were only six or eight weeks early. One woman in particular had just had twins, a boy and a girl, born about seven weeks early. Like Daddy and me, she had two older children. I told her how we'd lost Jonas and about your uncertain condition. *After* I told her about you and Jonas, she went on to say that she felt cheated because she'd had a caesarean.

Cheated? CHEATED?? Because she had to have a

Caesarean? I hope I didn't look as shocked as I felt. All I could think was, *Lady, they could have cut me open from my ankles clean up to my throat if it meant having both babies alive.*

Sunday, May 26, 2002

We stopped by the blood bank office Sunday morning, and the receptionist gave us a form to list people we would allow to donate for you. Only people on the list would be able to donate; only people with type O blood could be on the list. Your type was B-positive, but B-positive people could not donate for you at Hershey as at Reading. They would have had to do a "cross-match" and re-type your blood every three days if we wanted you to have B positive. If they gave you type O, they wouldn't have to re-type. We never did figure out why; but we were glad that Daddy and his parents, all type O, could now donate for you. And they could use the blood for twenty-eight days. As long as Daddy and Mom Mom and Pop Pop continued to rotate, there would always be blood for you.

They had already finished collecting blood for the day, and would be closed Monday for Memorial Day. Daddy couldn't donate blood before Tuesday morning. If you were still stable then, we planned to go home to get Patience and Owen after Daddy donated.

Later that day, Pop Pop phoned us in our room and gave Daddy a hard time about not having gone home for Patience and Owen yet. After Daddy got off the phone, he was upset, and I was in tears.

Pop Pop and Mom Mom had been at our apartment on

Saturday to give Grandma and Grandpa a break. Patience
and Owen, stressed out and unruly from all that had happened, were still fresh in his mind as he called to remind us
that "you still have responsibilities at home too."

And we had just been cautioned again that your condition could very likely deteriorate due to your lungs and
recent surgery. We did not feel comfortable leaving you
before Tuesday, when you should be past your most critical
days.

Pop Pop didn't seem to understand that you *needed* us
here. And until we felt more certain of your condition, we
felt we needed *each other* here. We didn't want to split up
and have one of us go home for Patience and Owen.

Nor did we feel comfortable with having Patience and
Owen with us at the hospital. What would we do in the case
of an emergency, and we had to make a decision about treatment options? We couldn't see trying to make any major
decisions about your care while trying to rein in two unruly,
stressed-out children. Nor did we like the option of one of us
staying back with Patience and Owen while the other went
to the hospital alone. We needed to stick together without
them for another two days.

I wondered if people thought we planned to leave
Patience and Owen with my parents all summer while we
"vacationed" in Hershey. "Can't he give us just a few days
to figure things out?" I bawled. "It's not like we're abandon-
ing our children!"

Daddy was frustrated and angry. "I guess we should
just go home for the rest of the summer and tell them to just

do what they gotta do with Hiram and FedEx him home when they're done!"

Pop Pop was right. And we were right. Patience and Owen needed us—but you needed us too. We had to strike an impossible balance.

We needed a plan to minimize our time apart from each other and apart from the children (Patience and Owen *and* you), to give us an occasional break from Patience and Owen, and to keep from overloading anyone else.

When we visited you a little later, we worked on a tentative weekly plan. We decided to go home each week from Monday morning to Tuesday afternoon and work for Grandpa to keep up with the rent. We asked Grandma to come to Hershey for a few hours each Thursday to watch Patience and Owen. We also asked Mom Mom and Pop Pop to come on Saturdays to help with Patience and Owen. We knew we'd need to tweak our plan a lot over the summer to suit everyone's needs, but at least we had a start.

Monday, May 27, 2002, Memorial Day

You never did look particularly bad just after your surgery. Your lungs stayed well within the NICU's medical capabilities. Your bowel drainage was slowing and the doctors hoped this meant the perforation was small and healing on its own, which would mean no further surgery. We had been worried about how such a small baby could possibly tolerate a major surgery. But once again, it looked like you would pull through and survive.

We had already learned to know a lot of the NICU staff,

but a nurse we hadn't met yet was taking care of you this morning.

"Hi. My name's Jeanne," she introduced herself. She was blond, fifty-something, and slightly shorter than I. She seemed very comfortable with you, with her job, with us, and with herself. I liked her immediately.

"Hiram's a very sick little boy," Jeanne continued, "so I decided to take him as my primary."

That meant that anytime Jeanne was working, she would take care of you. She'd be your main nurse. She could oversee things somewhat and give continuity to your NICU stay.

I nodded my head at the news, grateful to have Jeanne as your primary. I didn't think much more about Jeanne right then, but as the summer progressed, I thanked God for her often.

Later that day, Al and Pauline Menger stopped by to visit us on their way home from seeing their daughter and her family. Their son-in-law was a pastor and Al had preached from his pulpit yesterday. Al told us he had used *us* as a sermon illustration. He'd told the congregation he had some friends going through some really troubled waters, but that you'd never be able to pick us out in a crowd, because our countenances were still peaceful through it all.

Although we still felt a bit numb from the shock of losing Jonas, God was sustaining us. We could not have felt or acted peacefully without Him.

Tuesday, May 28, 2002

You were still stable, and past the days expected to be your worst. We visited you before we went to the blood donation center. After Daddy donated, we headed home for Patience and Owen. Grandma didn't tell them we were coming in case something derailed our plans. I called Patience and Owen from my cell phone when we were about a minute away and kept them on the phone with me until we pulled into the driveway.

Patience and Owen shrieked with joy when they saw us. We hadn't seen them since we'd put them to bed on Thursday, the day of Jonas's funeral.

Daddy knelt and held out his arms to Patience and Owen as they ran to him. It was beautiful to watch them and to be together again. Yet I knew it would be a long time until we could really *all* be together — with you too — if you ever did come home. But even then, we'd never in this life be a complete family, because Jonas was gone. The circle would always be broken.

As I watched your brother and sister climb all over Daddy, I wondered if you would ever be able to roughhouse like this. Or would you be too crippled by the brain bleed? Would you even survive to the end of the summer?

We told Patience and Owen all about the Ronald McDonald House — the playroom in the basement, the playground outside, and the snacks that were always set out on the kitchen counter. We wanted to get them enthused about the idea of living in an unfamiliar place. It worked. They could hardly wait to go.

Part Three

We spent time with Patience and Owen and took care of some personal business—such as getting our mail forwarded to RMH. We showed Patience and Owen the video we'd taken, to prepare them for how you looked. After supper, we packed some clothing and toys and left for Hershey.

Your nurse kindly waived the only-two-visitors-at-a-time rule so that all five of us could be together for this first visit. Patience and Owen were thrilled to reach into your isolette and touch the sole of your foot. They seemed very uninhibited. They looked right past all the tubes and wires and saw only their baby brother. This was a big plus about Hershey: Patience and Owen could visit you here. No children were allowed in the Reading NICU.

At this point I began sending daily e-mails to update friends and family about you. I had over sixty people on my mailing list by the end of the summer, and many of them forwarded my messages to others. I have no idea how many people received my updates.

Some people told us they eagerly checked their e-mail several times daily for Hiram updates. People felt connected to us as they read my updates, and they assumed the feeling was mutual. Yet few people responded. The one-way communication left us feeling cut off from everyone.

Chapter Fourteen

Wednesday, May 29, 2002

I went in to see you after the doctors had finished their rounds. Daddy stayed with Patience and Owen, so this was the first time I'd visited you by myself. Without Daddy to talk to and distract me, thoughts of Jonas came crashing in on me. I couldn't look at you without thinking of Jonas. I thought back to the delivery. Daddy and I had believed that you would both live. Or that you would both die. We had never imagined that one would live and one would die. You were identical twins. You belonged together. Yet here you were without Jonas.

I cried for Daddy's and my loss, and I cried for Patience and Owen's loss. But I cried for your loss most of all. I believe identical twins have a special bond, but now Jonas was gone and the bond was broken.

I wondered—since you started as one person, who was first? Or did the original person cease to exist when you divided into two? Or were you both somehow contained in the original person? And what about your souls? Before you became two, did you and Jonas share a soul? And how would you be affected now that you and Jonas didn't exist in the same realm anymore? Only God knew the answers.

The same thing happened to Daddy when he went to see you later. Dr. Michael saw Daddy with his head resting on your isolette and thought he was asleep. Daddy told Dr. Michael he was just thinking of you and Jonas and trying to shut out the rest of the world.

Daddy and I talked about it later. If only we had caught the TTTS earlier, maybe we could have done something. We knew that TTTS before twenty-four weeks is tantamount to a death sentence, so we were fortunate that even one of you survived. Yet we were frustrated not to have had the chance to do *something*. *If only we'd had that level 2 ultrasound,* I thought, *then we would have caught the TTTS earlier. We could have tried the laser surgery; I could have been on bed rest; we could have tried doing the reduction amnio before I'd gone into labor . . .* Even if Jonas had died despite all that, at least we would have known that we had tried. We wouldn't wonder as we did now. It was so incredibly *frustrating.*

But it was over now. Nothing could be undone or redone. Jonas was gone. No amount of questioning, research, or knowledge about TTTS would bring him back. Yet it would always be in the back of our minds—"What if?"

I determined not to have to ask "What if?" about you. If you died, it wouldn't be because of some oversight. Although the doctors and nurses had done a remarkable job with you so far, I was still skeptical. I'd lost a lot of faith in doctors. I went to the Penn State College of Medicine library and copied pages upon pages out of neonatology textbooks. I felt that if I had been more informed about twin-to-twin transfusion, I might have prevented all of this. I determined to be as informed as possible about your present condition so that no mistakes would happen again.

But less than a week later, the sheer volume of material proved more than I could handle. I still read a lot about your condition, but only to be informed, not to look over the doctors' shoulders. Besides, I told myself, this is Hershey — not Reading. I think Dr. Rosato missed the twin-to-twin because many women with normal twin pregnancies (if there is such a thing) have the same symptoms I had, and everything is fine. He saw no reason to believe my pregnancy would turn out any differently. Here at Hershey, you already were not a "normal" newborn. They *expected* problems with you and would stay on top of things.

Thursday, May 30, 2002

Daddy got up early to see you while I slept in with Patience and Owen. Then we all had breakfast and went for a drive. After the drive, I took my turn visiting you while Daddy pushed Patience and Owen in the double stroller around the hospital grounds.

When I asked your nurse how you were doing, she reported that your bowel drainage was still almost nothing, the exact amount was .4 cc. "You know — that would be a quarter of a cc," she said.

Oh, my, I thought, catching her math error, *this woman's taking care of Hiram?*

"So how long are you on today?" I asked.

"Till three," she answered.

Just a few more hours. Phew! That was a relief. Once I was sure no harm would come to you in the last few hours of your nurse's shift, I left the NICU to find Daddy, Patience, and Owen and head back to the House.

Lorinda came around 4:00 p.m. to visit us and watch the children so we could visit you together. We were refreshed by her visit. We shared with her our difficulties with Patience and Owen, who had been very poorly behaved since your birth. We were often at our wits' end to know what to do with them. We were stressed out and inconsistent with discipline, and they took advantage of it. In addition, we didn't want another House guest to report us if they saw or heard us spanking our children. We'd already lost Jonas. We didn't want to risk having our other children taken away, even if they were unruly meanwhile.

After Lorinda returned home that evening, she sent us an e-mail describing her experience with Patience and Owen:

Hi Wendy,

I wanted to tell you this cute little incident that happened tonight but didn't want to tell you in front of Patience. After she went to the bathroom, I gave them both instructions to stand outside of the bathroom and wait for me. I closed the door and fully expected them to wander down the hall, or go back to the playroom. When I came out, they were both standing there. It shocked me! My boys would have NEVER done that! I praised Patience for obeying me, and she replied, "Owen started walking away, but I spanked him." I almost laughed out loud over that! And, I didn't hear any squawks from Owen when I was in the bathroom, so I don't think the spanking was painful. Plus, I've survived with five siblings, and I know the human nature to want to discipline your fellow offspring. Anyhow, I wanted to tell you that even if your children are obnoxious and disobedient now, they're just working off their frustrations and misunderstandings. Their obedience today was a sign that their training really does kick in when Mom and Dad aren't around. And that was really neat for me to see. So, I just wanted to pass that on to you.

> With love,
> Lorinda

Friday, May 31, 2002

When Grandma and Grandpa visited today, they took their first picture of you. Your nurse, Felicia, agreeably lifted your isolette lid so they could snap a picture. Then while Grandma and Grandpa watched Patience and Owen at the House, Daddy and I went to see you.

Felicia was caring for you when we came into the NICU. She encouraged us with a story about an ex-preemie who went to her church. This girl had had massive Grade IV brain bleeds on both sides of her brain. She was now at the top of her seventh grade class and sang in the choir. Her only remaining "problem" was that she wore glasses.

Sunday, June 2, 2002

We visited Rob Ail's church this morning. We wanted to go where we knew someone.

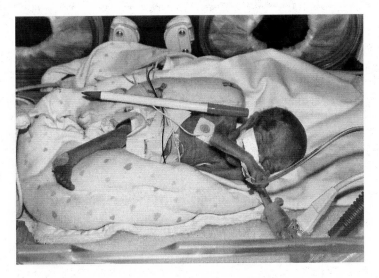

Hiram in the NICU. Note his size compared to the pen.

The sermon was titled "Till Death Do Us Part," and the pastor made it clear that divorce and remarriage were un-Biblical. Although it was about marriage, the title made me think about Jonas. Death had parted us.

The last time our family had been to church had been Mother's Day – six days before Jonas's death. That thought alone choked me up; but as I filled out the visitor's card, the tears flowed when I came to the section asking our children's names and ages. I included Jonas, noted that he was your twin; and for his age I put "deceased."

Daddy looked at me questioningly. Why was I crying? I showed him the place on the card where I filled in our children's names, and Daddy's face melted sympathetically.

"I'm sorry, Wen," he said. "I should have looked at that card. I should never have let you fill that out."

While I was with you Sunday afternoon, two women arrived in the NICU with their teenage daughters. They were at the hospital for a fund-raising event for the Children's Hospital. One of the girls, Anna, had been a preemie born at twenty-five weeks. She was a twin. Her sister hadn't survived.

I felt like a person in a desert who had just found water. Here was someone who could understand. I didn't know if I was more interested in talking to Anna's mother because we had such similar experiences, or if I wanted to talk to Anna about how she'd adjusted to being an only twin.

But Anna was more interested in Kyra, the baby beside you, than she was in either you or me. Anna's whole reason for coming to the NICU was to see a baby who was the same size she'd been at birth. And Kyra was almost exactly the size Anna had been at birth. With Kyra's mother's permission, Anna and her mother stepped near you and me to look at Kyra.

In my brief conversation with Anna, she said, "You always know you were a twin." Maybe she always sensed that part of her was missing. But when I asked if she and her sister were identical or not, she said, "I don't know. Mom? Were we identical?"

I was incredulous. How could you be thirteen years old and never have thought to ask if you were identical? That would have been one of my first questions. I'd have wanted to know if we would have looked the same, if we could have traded places, if I was the very image of my dead sibling.

Yet in another way it comforted me that Anna had never

asked that question. Her missing twin had obviously not left her with a burning emptiness that consumed her thinking. That laid to rest some of my concerns about how you might someday feel about not having Jonas — if you lived that long.

After they were gone I stood gazing at your face. I noticed that your eyes were just beginning to open. You and Jonas had been so premature that your eyes were still fused shut. When I told Daddy that one of your eyes was opening, he asked, "Which one?"

"The upper one," I answered, and Daddy gave me a strange look. Then I realized what an odd answer I'd given.

"Sorry, Russ," I said, laughing. "I meant the right eye."

You always lay with your head looking out to the side, never straight up, so that your breathing tube would stay in the proper place. I didn't think of your eyes as left and right, only up and down, depending which way your head was turned.

Monday, June 3, 2002

We did our usual Monday/Tuesday thing. Daddy got up early to visit you, and then we came home to a busy day of working in the barn to keep up with the rent. Grandma watched Patience and Owen in our apartment while we worked.

That afternoon, Daddy ran a long-overdue errand and collected the money that Verna Fry owed us for her newspaper delivery. Verna was an older lady whose sweetheart had died in WWII, and she had never married. But she didn't let that make her bitter. She had a beautiful spirit.

If we'd had a "most thoughtful comment" contest, Verna would have won. When Daddy explained why he wasn't running the route anymore, Verna said slowly, "Doesn't it make you wonder — why couldn't there just be one baby, and it be healthy?"

Why indeed? Daddy and I had both wondered what purpose there was in this. The Lord gives and the Lord takes away.

My friend Kristin came to visit that evening, bringing a gift for you. She'd just been in for a prenatal checkup with Dr. Rosato. Dr. Rosato told her that he'd been very impressed with how Daddy and I had handled ourselves in the wake of Jonas's death.

"Sure," I answered, " He probably says that about everybody."

"No," Kristin insisted, "he really meant it."

The conversation inevitably shifted to Dr. Rosato's competence. "Russ and I are seriously thinking of suing," I said.

Kristin was utterly shocked, but she tried to measure her words as we discussed the subject. She, as I, was loath to even consider that her beloved, trusted doctor could have messed something up.

I understood her shock. Daddy and I hated the thought of a lawsuit ourselves. People tend to be loyal to their doctors. But everyone who heard our story believed that malpractice had taken place — everyone except Kristin and another friend, also a patient of Dr. Rosato's. With so many family and friends feeling that we had a moral obligation to sue, Daddy and I were starting to resign ourselves to pursuing a lawsuit.

Once we had Patience and Owen in bed for the night, Daddy and I both had an overwhelming desire to go to Hershey to see if your eyes had opened any further. We would go to Hershey tomorrow anyway, but we felt we couldn't wait that long. Grandma agreed to stay in our apartment while we drove out to Hershey and back. We had been gone about twenty minutes when Grandma called my cell. Patience was awake and upset and shaking uncontrollably. Daddy and I abandoned our plans of a late-night visit with you, and turned around to go home to Patience.

When we arrived home, Patience was still awake and trembling. She seemed nauseated. We weren't sure if she was coming down with something, or if she had just had a very upsetting dream. Daddy slept on the recliner with Patience that night. She was fine the next morning. We concluded that she must have had a bad dream. This was the first of many such episodes Patience had that summer. Once she woke, she could never recall the dreams. Even Patience was showing symptoms of grief and stress.

Chapter Fifteen

Wednesday, June 5, 2002

My twenty-sixth birthday.

Dr. Dennis Mujsce (Myoose), the neonatologist on service the next two weeks, was very kind and compassionate. My voice broke while speaking to him. Embarrassed at my lack of composure, I mumbled, "I'm just trying not to think of Hiram's brother."

"Why?" he asked simply.

I didn't think it would be good for other parents' morale to see me bawling, but I was too near to tears to say so. I just shrugged my shoulders.

I was relieved when Dr. Mujsce moved from the sensitive topic of Jonas and updated me about you.

"We thought Hiram might just have a small perforation in his bowel," Dr. Mujsce explained, "and a lot of indications point to this being the case, but now there's also the possibility of a section of sick bowel. Every X-ray shows one loop of bowel that is always in the same place and always has air in it. That loop of bowel could be diseased or dead."

"Can he still recover if he does have a bad section of bowel?" I asked.

"Hiram can still recover from a section of sick bowel," Dr. Mujsce assured me, "but his prognosis is obviously going to be better if he *doesn't* have a bad section of bowel, and it's just a small perforation.

"Another big concern right now is Hiram's nutrition," Dr. Mujsce continued. "Since he isn't able to take anything by mouth, he's getting all of his feeds through the IVs. It's a delicate balance to give him enough nourishment to grow and heal, but not so much that it overtaxes his liver. Hiram's lungs are still doing okay for a preemie of his gestation."

"What would you say Hiram's chances of survival are now?" I hadn't asked this question since you were given odds of 80 percent at two days old and after coming to Hershey with your bowel perforation; I wasn't sure I wanted to know. I braced myself for Dr. Mujsce's answer.

"I'd say he has about a 50 percent chance," Dr. Mujsce answered.

Wow, I thought, *that's not bad odds for the smallest baby in the NICU.*

Great Mom Mom and Great Pop Pop (Grandpa's parents) stopped to visit us on their way home from a family reunion near Altoona. Daddy met them at the hospital and took them to see you. Great Mom Mom fell in love with you. She couldn't stop talking about how she'd seen you move your hand a few times. She felt a special kinship with you; her twin Walter had died about a year before.

Patience and Owen really enjoyed life at RMH. It's quite an accomplishment for someone to create a "home away from home" that even children love. They enjoyed the play-room in the basement, but we spent a lot of time upstairs too. Patience and Owen loved to watch the fish in the small aquarium in the living room. Their favorite was the "dotty fish" — a small black catfish with white speckles.

There were always other children to play with — like Abby, the two-and-a-half-year-old former preemie who was going to the feeding clinic; and Lydia, a five-year-old here for heart surgery. We enjoyed getting to know the other families who, like us, had found a temporary home at RMH.

Saturday, June 8, 2002

We looked at church listings in the local paper that night, hoping to find one that met in a school gym. Our home church also met in a gym, and we thought we'd feel at home in a similar setting. Two churches met that criterion. We decided to visit Light and Hope Fellowship.

Sunday, June 9, 2002

I wrote one sentence in my journal for this date: "Visited Light and Hope Fellowship today." This simple line doesn't do justice to our experience there.

Pastor Jim was a very tall, lean man, with graying brown hair and a close-cropped beard. His soft-spoken manner made me think he might have been better suited as a children's pastor. But after hearing him preach, I realized his gifts were well utilized right where he was. His humility and gentleness added power to his message.

Daddy filled out one of the prayer request slips, briefly explaining our story, and put it into the offering plate when it was passed. Pastor Jim took the slips and returned to the podium to publicly pray for each request. No one knew whose prayer request was whose.

After praying for several requests, Jim came to our slip: "I have a prayer request here for a baby who's four weeks old. He was born sixteen weeks early. He's here at Hershey for bowel surgery. There's a twin brother Jonas . . . Oh. It looks like Jonas died . . ."

My tears were never far from the surface, but I managed not to break into full-blown sobs when Pastor Jim mentioned Jonas's death.

We were astonished to have you prayed for on the spot. I had thought the slip would go to some prayer committee. We'd never before visited a church where we felt so instantly at home among fellow believers.

After the service, an attractive older woman named Nancy Husson introduced herself to us. She had a very sweet, kind nature. We shared our story with her.

She asked us, "What are your needs?"

She didn't ask, "Do you have any needs?" When people asked us that, we almost always responded, "No. We're fine. We don't need anything." Her question acknowledged that we had needs and confirmed that she truly wanted to know what they were. She wasn't asking the question just because etiquette demanded it.

Surprised, I paused a moment and then answered,

"Well, actually, our biggest need now is for someone to watch the children occasionally so Russ and I can go visit Hiram together."

Nancy was the secretary to the administrator of Hershey Medical Center and was currently on medical leave for ovarian cancer. She'd been through some troubled times. She'd just finished her last treatment and had one more week before returning to work.

She offered to watch Patience and Owen later that week and said she would try to organize others in the church to help once a week. I felt such a relief. *This is how it should be,* I thought. The body of Christ near Hershey, PA, was doing for us what our home church could not do.

Although our focus was on you that summer, the inspiration of Light and Hope encouraged us that our own struggling church could someday thrive like this.

Later that night, Daddy went to visit you while Patience and Owen and I slept. Around midnight, Patience had a particularly bad dream. Trembling uncontrollably, she breathed rapidly and mumbled nonsense. Trying to calm her down, I thought if I could just wake her up, maybe she'd snap out of it.

After a long ten minutes, I called the NICU and asked to talk to Daddy. Your nurse told me Daddy had left about twenty minutes before. That alarmed me. If Daddy had left the hospital twenty minutes ago, why wasn't he back in our room?

I tried to call Daddy's cell phone, but he didn't answer.

Now I really started to panic. Had something happened to Daddy? Had he been in an accident on the short drive from the hospital to the House? It was an irrational thought. Even if Daddy had been in an accident, I would have heard sirens. But after losing Jonas, part of me was bracing for another tragedy, and I assumed the worst.

Meanwhile, I put Patience in the bathtub. I ran the water a little cooler than usual, hoping it would help wake her up. It worked. I soon had her tucked back into her bed, sleeping soundly.

Now I was consumed with worry about Daddy. I got dressed, grabbed the baby monitor, and went downstairs to look for him. I found him in the kitchen munching cheese curls and chatting with another House guest. I felt tremendous relief, along with outrage that he had put me through all this worry.

"Why didn't you have your cell phone on? I've been trying to get you, and they said you left the NICU almost half an hour ago. I thought something happened to you!"

I must have looked wild-eyed and panicky. The other parent must have thought I was crazy.

Daddy pulled his phone out of his pocket and said simply, "Huh. What do you know? It *is* off. Sorry, Wen."

Chapter Sixteen

Monday, June 10, 2002

You were scheduled for an abdominal ultrasound later in the day to look at that loop of bowel that never moved. We weren't terribly worried though. This was your third day off the antibiotics, and you still showed no sign of recurring infection.

Confident that we would hear a good report about your bowels, we went home to get some work done for Grandpa after my early-morning visit with you. Grandma watched Patience and Owen in our apartment while Daddy and I worked together in the barn.

Late in the afternoon, my cell phone rang. It was Dr. Piscun, a surgical resident. He seemed confused that we were home and not at the hospital, which annoyed me. We'd told the nurses we were going home overnight. Did he think we were always at home and didn't care about you? Maybe he was just surprised that we had chosen that day to go home in light of what the doctors had told us about observing you as you finished your antibiotics. But we were

confident of your well-being and figured the doctors had
just been very cautious.

Dr. Piscun said you needed surgery again. The ultrasound had revealed a fluid-filled, infected section of bowel—
the same loop that had looked suspicious on the X-rays. This
was the surgery we'd been hoping to delay or even avoid.

Is Hiram big enough now, I wondered, *or do they have no
choice but to go ahead with the surgery?*

Dr. Piscun didn't seem worried. He just said that you
needed surgery. The plan was to drain the infection from
your bowel. If Dr. Cilley saw anything that needed fixing, he
would do that as well; but he didn't plan to go looking for
stuff to fix.

I asked Dr. Piscun to call back on our home phone so he
could explain the whole thing to Daddy. Meanwhile, I
explained it all to Grandma and Grandpa. Dr. Piscun told
Daddy they'd operate the next day. Grandma readily offered
to keep Patience and Owen so we could be together at the
hospital for your surgery.

That evening an anesthesiology resident called. Daddy
answered the phone.

"Hello," the resident sing-songed in a thick foreign
accent, "we are calling to get permission to give the anesthesia for your son's surgery."

"What's the name of the drug you'll be using?" Daddy
asked out of curiosity.

The resident named something Daddy had never heard
of before. "It is an inhalation anesthetic," he said. "We will
be giving it to him through his IV."

Right, Daddy thought, *an inhalation anesthetic given through an IV.*

"So will you be the one doing the anesthesia?" Daddy asked.

"Oh, no," the resident rambled on in his peculiar accent, "I will not be the one doing the anesthesia."

That's all I need to know, Daddy thought, and he gave permission for the anesthesia.

Daddy and I had a good laugh about the inhalation anesthesia in the IV. "Okay, veins," we joked, "take a deep breath!"

We must have truly been adjusting to life as the parents of a very sick preemie. This was the surgery we'd been dreading, but we didn't panic. We didn't even rush to your bedside that night. Although concerned by this latest setback, we calmly spent the night at home and calmly went to Hershey the next morning.

Tuesday, June 11, 2002

We visited with you and prayed over you as much as possible before the surgery and then left around 3:00 p.m. when the anesthesiologist came. On our way out, we crossed paths with Dr. Cilley.

"So is this another non-event, like the Penrose drain?" I asked hopefully.

Dr. Cilley looked at me very seriously. "Oh, no," he answered emphatically, "this is an *event.*"

Now we were grounded in reality. After sending a brief e-mail to let everyone know the surgery was beginning,

Daddy and I headed to the cafeteria for sandwiches to take with us to the waiting area. We knew it could be a long surgery, and we might get hungry. We also knew that if something went wrong, Dr. Cilley would want to speak to us immediately. Surprisingly, we weren't very nervous. In the beginning, every new medical problem sent adrenaline rushing though our veins. But as the weeks wore on, we seemed to develop emotional calluses; the ups and downs became almost mundane. Dealing with each new crisis simply became a way of life. Or maybe we just didn't have energy left to get worked up. Here we sat placidly munching sandwiches as the surgeons cut open our tiny son to see if they could once again save his life.

But we were anxious for word. After an hour or so, we moved from the waiting room to the bench in the hallway just outside the NICU so we could talk to Dr. Cilley the moment he stepped out.

My mind wandered to a true story I'd read some years before in *Reader's Digest* about a premature girl. She'd needed bowel surgery just like you. Before the operation, the surgeon had assured the parents that all the signs seemed to point to just a small section of dead bowel. They had waited calmly during the surgery just as we were now doing. It wasn't long before the surgeon had reappeared, ashen-faced, and told the parents, "The whole thing is necrotized."

There's no way to live with no bowel. They had held their daughter while she died. As I remembered this story, the waiting started to get to me. Would they tell us the same thing about you?

Finally, Dr. Cilley burst out of the NICU at his usual brisk pace. Spotting us, he began explaining in his clear, forthright manner exactly what he had done and how it had gone.

"The surgery went well. Hiram did well. I removed a section of dead bowel. There were some patchy, questionable sections downstream from the part I removed, but I left that alone."

Dr. Cilley had made a new incision down the middle of your belly, right over your belly button. Dr. Cilley explained that the dead section had been at about the halfway point of the small intestine. Because of the questionable areas downstream, he did not splice the bowel back together. Instead, he brought the loose end of the healthy upstream bowel to the surface, attaching it to your left-side incision where the Penrose drain had been. This was your ostomy. You could still be fed by mouth and pass stool through the healthy section of your bowel, but you would need an ostomy bag over the ostomy to catch your stool. Dr. Cilley had also brought the loose end of the questionable downstream section to the surface and attached it to the right-side incision where the other end of the Penrose drain had been. He hoped that the downstream section would heal itself so that he could eventually splice your bowels back together. The drain tube was, of course, gone. Since the dead, leaking section of bowel was now removed, there was no longer anything to be drained.

With such a short upstream section of bowel, it would be hard for you to absorb enough nutrition. You might still have to depend on IVs for a lot of your nutrition.

Part Three

Thursday, June 13, 2002

E-mail:

Hiram is looking a little more comfortable today. He's been urinating better, so he's not quite so puffed-up looking. His blood pressure is better too (it had been too low).

I was in to see Hiram at about 8:30 this morning. I knew I could only stay till 9 because the docs do rounds from 9 to 11 and they don't allow visitors in the NICU during rounds.

Just before 9 the ultrasound tech rolled his machine in to do an ultrasound for Hiram. Premature babies usually have lower blood oxygen levels and other signs of distress when they're disturbed (like during ultrasounds and diaper changes and stuff) and it helps them if Mom or Dad is around to place a hand on the top of their head during the procedure. So I thought I'd push my luck and stay until I got kicked out. The docs were starting at the other end of the unit so I thought maybe no one would notice me.

Then Hiram's nurse came up and put her hand on my shoulder. I looked at her and said, "Time for me to go?" and took my hand off Hiram's head.

And she said, "You might want to stay here with your hand on his head till the ultrasound is done. It'll probably help keep him more stable."

I was so grateful that I almost cried. I thought to myself, okay Wen, let's get a grip here or the ultrasound tech is really going to think you're weird. *It's so easy to feel like he's the hospital's baby and not my baby. Those of you who've had a baby in the NICU will know what I'm talking about. Jonas felt more like my baby than Hiram does — I guess because I got to hold Jonas for the whole day before we gave him to the nurse to be taken to the*

131

morgue. Even though he was dead, I felt more like Jonas's mother than I feel like Hiram's mother. So I guess that's why I was so touched by being allowed to stay with Hiram during the ultra-sound. His nurse said he did really well throughout the ultrasound — his O^2 level stayed up pretty well.

He's looking about as good as he can look for one who just had surgery two days ago.

But he's not out of the woods yet. As Russ would say, he's still pretty deep in the woods — he's got a whole summer's worth of woods to go yet. But so far so good. He's had some hurdles to get over and he's done them all so far. Thanks for all your continued prayers and encouragement. Every prayer and every encouraging e-mail counts.

Wendy

I got back from your ultrasound around 9:30 a.m. Daddy and I were eating breakfast with Patience and Owen when Pastor Jim arrived. We talked at the dining room table until 11:30, discussing all manner of things pertaining to our situation, mostly details of all that had happened to this point and our struggles over suing.

"I really wish I could just talk to Dr. Rosato and get his take on all that happened before Hiram and Jonas were born," I told Jim. "But how can you get any straight answers out of doctors these days? They're all too worried about being sued."

Jim promised to try to locate a Christian doctor for me to talk to. He said he knew a Christian lawyer as well but was not sure whether he handled malpractice cases. Jim had connections to so many people. We were glad to have him working on our side.

Friday, June 14, 2002

Nancy Husson came to watch Patience and Owen around 10:30 a.m. We planned to visit you beginning at 11:00, so this gave Patience and Owen time to get used to her before we left. Nancy gave them both dolls. The dolls, plus Nancy's sweet, gentle personality, instantly won them over. They didn't fuss at all when we left.

Chapter Seventeen

Saturday, June 15, 2002

I visited you for about three hours before rounds. As I often did, I helped Jeanne do your care. I took your temperature, changed your diaper, and lifted you up in your isolette while Jeanne changed your bedding.

Then Jeanne asked if I wanted to give you a sponge bath. I couldn't believe I'd be allowed to do that. She set me up with the bath supplies, gave me a few basic instructions, and told me she'd be nearby if I needed anything. There was no hovering or critiquing my method. Jeanne was always wonderful that way. She made me feel like you were really my baby. I loved giving you that bath. Even though I had to be careful of the tubes and wires, it felt like such a normal mothering activity.

When I arrived back at the House, Patience and Owen were especially difficult. And it was raining. The dreary day depressed me, and my elation over giving you a bath faded. There seemed to be no escaping the unruliness of our older children or your endless medical problems.

Part Three

Lorinda and her husband Art had planned to visit around 11:00. *If we can just make it till eleven,* we thought. We began eagerly watching for Art and Lorinda around 10:50. By 11:15, we wondered if they were coming. At 11:30, a voice on the intercom announced a phone call for the Boyds. It was Art saying they wouldn't be coming after all. Lorinda had a cold. It was just a minor case of the sniffles, but they knew the risks to you if we got infected with it. We could pass the cold to you before we knew we had it, or we might have to stop visiting you for a few days while we were sick. Although grateful for their good sense not to come with a cold, we were terribly disappointed. We felt like we'd never get through that day.

Although we had planned to visit you together after Art and Lorinda came, neither of us went right away after they cancelled. Patience and Owen behaved so poorly and demanded so much attention that neither of us wanted to abandon the other to face the drudgery alone.

After lunch the sky cleared, which lifted our spirits. I tried taking a nap with Patience and Owen while Daddy went to visit you. I figured I could handle being left alone with the children as long as we were all sleeping.

Jeanne was out on a baby transport while Daddy visited. As he left the hospital, he overheard some employees saying the transport was to land soon. Knowing they must be talking about Jeanne's baby transport, Daddy hurried back to RMH to bring us all back to the hospital. I hadn't seen any baby transports land; and since you had been brought in by helicopter, I really wanted to see how it was done.

135

We heard the distinctive "thud, thud, thud" of Life
Lion's rotors. As it got closer, we heard the same shrill
whine we'd heard at Reading when Life Lion had taken you
to Hershey. The sound wasn't quite as spectacular as I'd
remembered — probably because it wasn't 3:00 in the morning, and we weren't surrounded by buildings on three sides
to bounce the sound around — but it still pumped adrenaline
through my veins.

"Dat's Iram's baby owibopter," Owen said. Every helicopter was a baby helicopter. Ever since you had come to
Hershey, Owen said those same words every time he saw a
helicopter, thinking that helicopters did nothing more than
fly sick babies around.

Soon Jeanne and the respiratory therapist emerged with
the transport isolette — probably the same isolette they'd
used to bring you. They pushed the isolette around the
corner of the emergency area and disappeared.

When I visited you later that day, I saw the new
arrival in bed twenty-three — exactly where you had
started out. The baby looked so tiny! You had been the
smallest baby in the NICU up until now. This new baby
looked small enough to take that distinction from you. I
asked a nurse how small the baby was, and she replied
kindly that she wasn't allowed to tell me, but I could certainly ask her parents if I wanted. I ducked my head in
embarrassment. In my curiosity, I'd forgotten about privacy. Later I asked a nurse if she could say if you were no
longer the smallest baby. The nurse hesitated a second
and then confirmed that you were not. My heart ached as

I said a quick prayer for this tiny person and her family.

Sunday, June 16, 2002

When I visited you before church, your nurse Kelly told
me that your belly had swollen, causing your midline incision to split open. I asked if I could see it and was surprised
that Kelly agreed. I tiptoed to your isolette and peered cau-
tiously at your wound as she peeled back the piece of gauze
on top. The wound looked very open and pussy. I could see
all the way to your smooth muscle wall. Kelly said the surgeons would come to look at it sometime today. They'd
decide then if they wanted to re-stitch you, or just pack your
wound with gauze and allow it to heal from the inside out.

Kelly's shift ended at 7:00 a.m. Jeanne would take care of
you until 7:00 that night. We were glad to have two of our
favorite nurses taking care of you that day.

Before I left, I asked Jeanne about the open wound. She
explained that it didn't lower your chances of survival, but it
was still a setback because it would take longer to heal.

It was also the end of your belly button. Dr. Cilley's note
on your surgery reads that he had stitched you together in
such a way to give a "nice appearance of a neonate umbilicus." Now that you'd popped your stitches, the fake
"neonate umbilicus" was gone.

Sometimes I felt an urge to get away and be alone with
Christ. I was reading my Bible and praying for you, but it
sometimes felt artificial—like something done out of mere
habit. My times alone with God were just hurried moments

stuffed between visits with you and time spent with Patience and Owen and Daddy.

My prayers felt the same way. Since Jonas's death and your hospitalization I had felt spiritually paralyzed. I didn't doubt God's existence or love. I knew He was still there and that He cared. Yet my prayers consisted mostly of begging God to let you live. I seldom had the spiritual energy left to pray for other things, like for special wisdom to deal with Patience and Owen. I felt like I was clinging to the hem of Jesus' robe. My fingers held on with all their might. I could not for one second let go. As numb as I felt, I knew Jesus was the only Rock to whom I could anchor.

It didn't seem that we were really growing spiritually; but when Daddy and I later looked back on this time, we realized that we had grown. That summer was like the "hardening off" process in plants. Growers often expose their indoor seedlings to increasing amounts of sun, heat, and cold (and decreasing amounts of water) in the spring so they can be transplanted to the garden.

Perennials also harden off naturally in the fall to prepare for winter. All growth stops as the plant hunkers down to endure the cold days ahead. The plant looks miserable. Yet if one took "mercy" on a plant at this stage and gave it more warmth and some fertilizer, it would likely die over the winter.

Our time in Hershey was like that. Although we saw no obvious spiritual growth during this summer, God was laying the groundwork for us to be more deeply rooted in Him so that we could spiritually flourish later.

I had always expected to feel closer to God during a time of trial. It didn't work that way, but I was too busy and too distracted with you to dwell on it much.

I believe even righteous Job felt distanced from God during his trials. Yet he still clung to God and did not deny Him.

One day I finally yielded to God's Spirit and walked across a parking lot to a lonely spot next to a quiet woods. The only sound came from the summer bugs singing in their rounds from treetop to treetop.

I didn't do or say much, but it was a wonderful time of fellowship with God. There was no pressure to visit you, no pressure to be with Daddy and Patience and Owen. I sat and wept over all that had happened, and God comforted me. I cried tears of grief, but also tears of refreshment. I felt like a hot, tired, thirsty traveler who had just found a small water-fall to stand under. I could drink and be refreshed and cooled and cleansed.

This experience wasn't an instant "fix" for my spiritual numbness; but it *did* remind me that God was with us, even when He seemed far away. It was as though God was saying to me, "I know, daughter. I know this is tough. I'm with you. I'll carry you. We'll get through this together."

I've been so thankful since for that time near the woods with God. He could have allowed me to keep plugging wearily on; but instead He called me away to refresh my weary soul.

Chapter Eighteen

Monday, June 17, 2002

We got to see the parents of the new baby in bed twenty-three. They looked so young; and they were Hispanic. I made a very racist assumption that they were a couple of teens with a baby. I found out later that the baby's name was Treasure Gonzales; her parents, Hector and Erica, were older than I.

Treasure had the same bowel disease you had. Since your surgery last week, we could no longer tell your X-rays by the safety pins. Now Treasure was the one whose X-rays had the safety pins. Her medical history was so similar to yours that the surgical residents nicknamed her "Hiram's twin." You were just as far along and almost the same birth weight. The only differences were that Treasure had not been a twin, and she'd had no major brain bleeds. She'd been born prematurely because of some major complications when Erica had appendicitis during her pregnancy.

I felt an instant kinship with Erica — along with a sense of shame for my racism. She and Hector were the kindest people. Our friendship deepened throughout the summer.

Later that day we went home to work for Grandpa
again. As Daddy helped Grandpa install their air conditioners, we talked about whether or not to keep my six-week
postpartum appointment with Dr. Rosato, scheduled for July
1. Grandpa didn't think I should. A friend had recently sent
me an e-mail saying she had a very uneasy feeling about me
returning to Dr. Rosato's office. We'd also talked to one of
my professors from school, and he'd said, "My insides are
just screaming that you shouldn't go."

Daddy wavered. He knew how desperately I wanted to
discuss your premature birth with Dr. Rosato; but he also
saw some wisdom in what everyone else was saying. When
Daddy decided I should cancel my appointment, I escaped
down the hill to the creek. I had to get away to come to grips
with his decision.

After they finished with the air conditioners, Daddy and
Grandpa came looking for me. It was out of character for me
to walk away like that, and they were worried.

"Go away," I called out from my hiding place in the
weeds, "I just want to be alone."

Grandpa left, but Daddy called to me again. I came out.

"It's just so unfair," I cried. "I understand what you all
are saying, and it makes sense not to go back, but I just want
to *talk* to him! And I guess you're right too, that I wouldn't
get any straight answers either, because he's probably
worried about getting sued. But it's not *fair!* We don't even
want to sue. We just want answers. But our culture is so

lawsuit-happy. So then we have to sue too—just to get those answers—and then we're just one more person who's sued a doctor."

Daddy listened patiently as I rambled on. He felt the same way, only he wasn't so emotional.

We ultimately decided to *reschedule* my appointment with Dr. Rosato for August 2. I wanted so desperately to question him. There had to be some reason that the TTTS had been missed, and I just wanted to know the reason. I also scheduled a postpartum checkup with a Hershey obstetrician, on August 26. Daddy and I could decide later which appointment to keep.

We also went to see some lawyers. The lawyers had to satisfy two criteria before proceeding with a lawsuit: 1) They had to first prove that my doctors had not met the standard of care. 2) They had to prove that the outcome would have been different (better) if the doctors *had* met the standard of care.

I asked one of the lawyers what he thought of my going back to Dr. Rosato for my postpartum checkup. He answered carefully, making it clear that I should have a checkup somewhere, but saying it might look funny if I were trying to sue my doctor, yet still trusted him enough to go back. The lawyer also said that it was pretty pointless to question Dr. Rosato because I probably wouldn't get straight answers, and it would simply prompt him to call his malpractice insurance company to give them a heads-up about me.

Part Three

Thursday, June 20, 2002

E-mail:

We don't really have any updates on Hiram today.

I just wanted to ask you all to pray for Russ and me as we deal with our four-year-old daughter Patience and our two-year-old son Owen. They've both been really difficult since this all started a month ago. And of course we're already stressed. Without going into any details, we are both burned out, exhausted, and at our wits' end with them. We even sleep in the same room with them here in Hershey, so we're constantly together except when we're at home, or when my mom is here to watch them. Russ's parents help too. I don't think we'd be sane without that, but we still need lots of prayer. Thanks!

Wendy

We had spoken to a friend about our struggles with Patience and Owen, and he pointed us to 1 Thessalonians 5:14: "Warn them that are unruly, comfort the feebleminded, support the weak, be patient toward all men."

Our most difficult task was to determine when they were truly brokenhearted over all that had happened, and when they were simply being unruly. Often, it was a combination of both, making it tough to sort out. Sometimes Patience would sit on her bed and cry.

"Why are you crying, Patience?" we would ask.

"I'm crying because Jonas died," she would wail.

Usually we believed her, but other times we suspected her of using a tried-and-true excuse to fuss. Meanwhile, we tried to plan some family outings to divert Patience and

Owen's attention from your hospitalization, and to provide some sense of normalcy.

Monday, June 24, 2002

You finally passed some stool from your stoma two days in a row. The doctors wanted to see a little more before feeding you by mouth, but at least your bowels were starting to work. On the other hand, your lungs were worse, and you were back to 100 percent oxygen. Plus it was Monday — the day we always went home to work.

When Grandma mentioned how nice it must be to get home sometimes, I shared my frustration. "We don't come home to relax," I said. "We come home to work. I hate coming home. It's the one job I feel like we can't quit."

Grandma was surprised. She and Grandpa had never considered it that way before. Later that evening, Grandma told us not to worry about working in the barn for the rest of your hospital stay. She said we could defer the rent until you came home. After that we didn't come home to work.

That night your oxygen level dropped, even though your ventilator was at 100 percent. It was bad enough that they called the neonatologist on call in the middle of the night, but not quite bad enough for them to call *us* in the middle of the night. The doctor adjusted your ventilator settings, and your sats were acceptable, but still not great, the rest of the night.

Tuesday, June 25, 2002

When we arrived back at RMH, it was good to know

that the next time we went home, it would be because we wanted to — not because we had to. Patience and Owen were excited to be back at the House again. They raced over to the aquarium to watch the fish as soon as we got in the door.

After a few seconds I heard Patience call, "Mommy, where's the dotty fish?"

I came over to check. The dotty fish liked to hide in the fake weeds, but after a few minutes of looking, I still couldn't find it. The dotty fish must have died while we were away. *Oh, God,* I prayed silently, *they've already lost Jonas. They may also lose Hiram. Please don't let the dotty fish die too. They've had enough to deal with.* My heart felt heavy with the idea of my children having to face the loss of their beloved dotty fish on top of everything else. If it didn't turn up in a day or so, I was tempted to sneak over to Wal-Mart and buy another fish like it and put it into the tank. We looked several more times that evening, with no sign of the dotty fish.

The next morning after breakfast, we checked the tank again. There was the dotty fish, swimming happily as though nothing had ever happened. Patience and Owen squealed with delight. I breathed a quick prayer of thanks to God.

Chapter Nineteen

Friday, June 28, 2002

Dr. Marks, the neonatologist on service for the next two weeks was South African, like Dr. Palmer. His very wavy, light brown hair gave him a wild, bushy look. I could almost picture him going off on a safari. But his serious face convinced me there was nothing wild or bushy about him. We'd liked all the other neonatologists, but this doctor really impressed us.

"Your son is very complicated," Dr. Marks explained in his crisp accent, "because so many major organs are involved."

At my request, he listed all the organs and their problems: 1) Your blood pressure was still low. Dr. Marks explained that you might still have poor vascular tone (Daddy called this "floppy veins"). 2) You had suffered a significant brain bleed, which could still result in water on the brain. 3) Because of your short upstream section of bowel you still received most of your feeds though the IVs, which was hard on your liver. 4) You'd been getting infections.

5) Your lungs still needed substantial ventilator support.

Dr. Marks was particularly concerned about your nutrition. "I'm *desperate* to feed Hiram," he told us.

You were getting a lot of fentanyl, which can slow digestion. The neonatologist previously on service had wanted you completely off the fentanyl and on lower ventilator settings before starting feeds. Dr. Marks simply looked at your chart and asked sharply, "Why is he getting so much fentanyl?" And then he decided to start small feeds that day as you were weaned from the fentanyl, rather than waiting.

Until Dr. Marks told us, we hadn't realized that fentanyl is a narcotic fifty times stronger than morphine. All this time I'd thought the stuff was more like heavy-duty baby Tylenol. Dr. Marks cautioned us that you might experience some withdrawal symptoms. Narcotics are stored in body fat, so the fact that you were so scrawny may have actually been in your favor this time.

Dr. Marks gave us an example of how you were complicated. He wanted to give you a medication to help with something—I forget if it was for your lungs, or your withdrawal from fentanyl or what. But this medicine had the tendency to lower blood pressure, and yours was already too low. We ran into many such roadblocks because of the many problems in your little body. The risk-to-benefit ratio of any treatment was very difficult to calculate.

I'll always remember what one nurse practitioner said without realizing that I was within hearing: "Yeah, that Hiram—he's a real mess!"

Saturday, June 29, 2002

As he'd promised, Dr. Marks began small feeds. Aside from the trophic feed at Reading, this was the first you'd received any milk. It was only one cc, which is one-fifth of a teaspoon; but it was a start. You weighed 2 pounds 1 ounce at this point. We hoped to soon increase both the amounts and the frequency of feedings and eliminate the IV nutrition.

Daddy and I developed a routine for visiting you. I would get up around 4:30 a.m., go to the NICU and stay until 9:00, when the doctors began rounds. Then I'd come back to eat breakfast with Daddy and Patience and Owen, and we'd spend time together until lunch. After lunch one of us would take a nap with Patience and Owen while the other visited you for another hour or two. Sometimes I'd take Patience or Owen over in the late afternoon to see you. We'd have supper and more family time in the late afternoon and evening. Daddy and I would have a prayer time with Patience and Owen before going to bed. Patience would pray every night in her four-year-old innocence, "Dear Lord, I pray for Hiram that You help his lungs and his bowels and his brains to get better. Amen." She loved you right from the start. Then I would go to sleep with Patience and Owen while Daddy visited you. He would usually get there around 9:00 or 10:00 and stay until midnight or 1:00 a.m.

When we added up the hours, we realized that we put in more than a full-time week with you. That was why we had quit our other jobs. You and Patience and Owen were our job that summer.

Part Three

Sunday, June 30, 2002

When I visited you in the morning, your lungs seemed
to have taken a turn for the better. Your oxygen was turned
back to 31 percent! You had improved so much that we
might even get to hold you for the first time that evening.

The nurse had to turn up your oxygen some when she
"did your care" — changing your diaper, suctioning your
breathing tube, and repositioning you; but that was normal.

You seemed a little jittery from the fentanyl withdrawal,
so I stayed with you until you fell asleep. Then I hurried
back to help Daddy get Patience and Owen ready for church.

When I got back to the House, I found Daddy and
Patience and Owen still asleep. *Doesn't Russ have the good
sense to at least make sure everyone is awake in time for church?* I
wondered irritably. *Do I have to do everything?* Of course, I
didn't have to do everything. Daddy often did more than
his share of work. Even though I'd just gotten such good
news about your oxygen, the stress of the summer and the
lack of sleep were getting to me. We ended up putting dry
cereal into cups for Patience and Owen to munch on the
way to church.

On one of the back roads on the way to Light and Hope,
a small bird flew in front of our car. I heard it hit below the
grille. It sounded loud enough that I assumed the bird died.
It made me think of Jonas, whose name means "dove." He
had died, just like the little bird.

When we headed back to the House after church, I
looked out my window as we neared the place where we
had hit the bird. Sure enough, the lifeless bird lay on the

side of the road.

When we got back to the House, I tried to shake off my
gloomy thoughts of Jonas and the bird. We needed to remain
positive. You were turned back up to 100 percent oxygen
again that night.

Jeanne had tentatively planned to let us hold you for the
first time tonight, but your high oxygen setting cancelled
those plans because your oxygen level would drop whenever anything stressful or different happened. Being held
would definitely be different.

Wednesday, July 3, 2002

A nurse had suggested that we request a conference
with all the health professionals involved in your care, since
you'd been in the hospital so long and were so complicated.
We did, and this was the day of the conference. Dr. Marks
was there, as well as Jeanne, Daddy and I, a respiratory therapist, and a social worker. We were glad for this opportunity, but part of me dreaded this conference. You seemed to
be making no progress. You were nowhere near full feeds;
your lungs continued to require almost 100 percent oxygen;
and you'd been getting infections in your blood.

What if Dr. Marks wanted to discontinue care because
he thought you were headed down an inevitable path to
death? What would we do then? That was the decision I
always dreaded. It had been bad enough when Dr. Brown
had asked if we wanted to discontinue care because of the
extreme likelihood of your being handicapped. It would be
even worse to face the possibility of discontinuing care

because of extreme likelihood of your death. The entire time
I braced myself for that awful question.

Dr. Marks said you were definitely making progress,
though very slowly. He said three things could still be
potentially fatal: 1) The chronic lung disease could worsen to
the point where your lungs stopped functioning. 2) As your
lungs healed, scar tissue could stiffen your lungs and cause
your heart to work too hard; and your heart could fail. 3)
You could have a recurrence of infection.

One reason your nutrition was so important was
because of your lungs, which needed nutrition so they could
heal and you could grow. You were up to one cc of milk
every three hours. Dr. Marks planned to double that either
this day or the next. You'd also been totally off the fentanyl
for about two days at this point. Overall, Dr. Marks gave you
better than a 50 percent chance of survival. He stressed that
your condition was still considered critical, but stable.

I could hardly believe it when the conference ended with
no mention of discontinuing your care. Dr. Marks, the respiratory therapist, and the social worker left the room first. I
started choking up with tears, which puzzled Daddy and
Jeanne since nothing new had been discussed. I was just so
relieved *not* to have had anything new or different. I shared
my fear that we would face a "pulling the plug" decision
someday. Jeanne just assured me that we were nowhere near
that point with you.

The "potentially fatal" list Dr. Marks had recited
included nothing we didn't already know. We always had a
vague sense that you could die at some point, and we

always talked about "if" you came home and not "when." As long as you were stable, we didn't allow ourselves to be consumed by fear of your dying. But we didn't get excited about your eventual homecoming either. We were emotionally guarded.

I can't attribute this calmness to strength of character on our parts. A lot of it was God sustaining us when we didn't even realize it, and part of it was that we were too wrung out to get upset about it. We didn't even have the energy to grieve Jonas, let alone to worry excessively about you. We didn't even feel that we had much energy to pray. We only hoped other faithful Christians were praying for us.

Thursday, July 4, 2002

In the evening we went to a friend's house for the Fourth of July. Grandma and Grandpa had been invited also. We enjoyed fellowshipping with old friends and feeling for a few hours like our lives were normal.

Chapter Twenty

Friday, July 5, 2002

Your lungs had gotten a lot worse since our conference two days before. Your chest X-ray looked awful, and your CO_2 was really high. Liz, the nurse practitioner, said it could be a simple matter of needing a diuretic, or it could be pneumonia. She said you'd probably need a tracheotomy at some point.

"We just had our conference with Dr. Marks on Wednesday," I said, "and he said Hiram was making progress, even though it was really slow. Are we no longer making progress?" I hated bad news, but I felt I had to have the answer to that question.

Liz hesitated a moment. She hated giving bad news as much as I hated getting it. "Hiram is no longer making progress," she finally answered.

The rest of July continued in much the same pattern. Slow progress, then a setback. Slow progress, then a setback. Slow progress, then a setback.

Months later, just before your discharge, a nurse named

Becky told me she had gone on vacation for three weeks in July. She had expected you to either go home or die before she returned. Becky returned to find that neither had happened. When she saw you were still languishing in the same condition — no better and no worse than when she left — she thought, *This isn't good.*

Daddy and I were dispirited at Liz's news, but we had a bright spot when we received an e-mail from Mike, a friend of Daddy's who was a part-time pastor. He'd started a benevolence fund for us at his church and wondered if we had any bills that the fund could pay for us. We'd also gotten back a $3,000 bond that we'd had to pay to the newspaper when Daddy had first begun his paper route. This was God's way of providing for us despite having no income that summer.

Later that day, you began some slow improvements again, but Daddy and I still faced other discouragements.

E-mail:

Hiram is doing better now. His CO_2 is back down to an acceptable level, so we're hoping that it was only fluid retention and that he won't end up with pneumonia. His ventilator is set to 63 percent oxygen, so that's better too. We may actually get to hold him tomorrow, but I'm not getting my hopes up. Please pray for Russ and me too. All of these ups and downs are really wearing us out.

There were also two sets of twin boys born this week who came up to the NICU, so that's been really tough. The one set was due two weeks before ours were and they're also identical just like ours.

Part Three

Their mother and Russ and I talked briefly as we stood between their isolettes and for just a second I imagined that they were mine. I just wanted to know what it felt like — just for one second — to have both of them. Russ said he did too — just for a second.

The twins' parents were in later again. The mom was holding one twin and the dad was holding the other. I just sat there with my hand in the isolette on Hiram's head and cried. It was so beautiful to watch the parents there with their two boys; but it was so sad, too, because it's something we'll never have.

It's really hard not to feel cheated. This is probably the toughest week we've had emotionally up to this point. Even the first week was easier than this because we had so much support from people that first week. We just feel so disconnected from everyone up here.

In case any of you have wanted to call or send a note but didn't have our numbers or address, I'm going to include them on the bottom of the e-mail. To all of you who have visited us, called us, sent e-mails or sent cards, thank you. You'll never know how uplifted we've been by you.

Wendy

In a situation like ours, each day feels much longer than twenty-four hours. It didn't take long for the positive effect of our Fourth of July picnic to wear off. We needed constant encouragement. Now we had no other outings or plans to look forward to — just an endless, dark summer stretching out ahead of us.

Although the pediatric floor of the hospital was full of people who had it worse than we did, the identical twins

I mentioned in my e-mail were still very difficult for us emotionally to observe. The other twins were fraternal and didn't bother me nearly as much. Their parents were Mennonite, and we got acquainted. During one conversation, I discovered they knew people we knew.

"Are your parents Mennonite?" Amy inquired curiously.

"No," I answered quickly.

Yet it had to be obvious to these people that I had some sort of Mennonite connection. I began feeling conspicuously underdressed in my shorts and snug-fitting, ribbed T-shirt.

As Daddy and I observed different families in the NICU and at the House, the Mennonite families consistently had the most support. Even in our own situation, we got a lot more support from my Mennonite friends than from our home church.

Daddy was especially intrigued by the Mennonites. In high school I had been convinced they were right, and my parents had agreed to send me to a Mennonite school for my last two years. Daddy had interacted with my friends at class reunions, dinner invitations, weddings, and an occasional visit to a friend's church. He had seriously considered that they may be right about a lot of things, but we were committed to our church.

Meanwhile, we agreed that I should rummage through my wardrobe for more modest clothing. I found several long, full skirts, some blouses, and a long dress. I didn't wear the shorts and T-shirt again.

Part Three

Although we didn't have support from our home church, we were building an emotional support network with nurses and the other parents at Hershey. I knew the nurses so well that I could close my eyes and name all of them by the sounds of their voices.

We were also close to the Ronald McDonald House staff — especially Todd Layser (the manager) and his wife Clara. Todd and Clara were Christians, and very welcoming and friendly.

During one conversation, Clara started to tell us a story about "two twins."

"As opposed to three twins?" Todd joked with her.

"Or as opposed to one twin?" Daddy asked wistfully. He was thinking of you without Jonas.

Chapter Twenty-One

Sunday, July 7, 2002

On the way to Light and Hope this morning, we hit another bird. This one didn't hit as hard as the one last week—more of a glancing blow. I looked back and saw the stunned bird feebly flapping its wings by the side of the road.

Last week's bird and this week's bird looked the same. Identical—just like you and Jonas. Would the bird live? Would you live? The two seemed connected. I could hardly wait for church to end so I could look for the bird. Yet part of me didn't want to know.

On the way home, there was no sign of the bird. It must have recovered and flown off.

Your oxygen setting of 70 percent was low enough that Jeanne said we could hold you. I sat in a rocking chair and unbuttoned the top of my shirt. Jeanne disconnected the breathing circuit from your ET tube and laid you on my chest so that your skin touched mine. Then I closed my shirt back over you, and Jeanne reconnected your breathing circuit and fastened it to my shirt to keep it steady. The skin-to-skin contact, plus the shirt over you, kept you warm outside your incubator. This was called "kangarooing."

What an incredible feeling to finally hold you after seven weeks! At only 2½ pounds, you had looked small in your incubator, but you felt even smaller as I held you. It was such a thrill to feel your warm little self cuddled up against me.

That week went better for you. Your oxygen requirements steadily decreased, and we increased to 5 ccs of breast milk every three hours. Full feeds would have been 23 ccs every three hours — we had a long way to go. Your feeds were increased very slowly because of absorption problems in your short section of bowel; but at least we were moving forward.

It was a difficult week for the rest of our family. Daddy took Patience and Owen home for the week for a break from RMH. I felt a strange mixture of giddiness and sorrow. Without the children, I could turn the lights on in the morning without waking anyone, and I could visit you as long as I wanted. I'd have more freedom than I'd had since Daddy and I were married. But as I watched our black Caravan taking Daddy and Patience and Owen away from me, a loneliness settled over me.

That week I averaged about ten hours a day in the NICU. I enjoyed your nurses and the other NICU parents almost as much as I enjoyed being with you. This was not the cold, impersonal hospital I had expected.

Wednesday, July 10, 2002

Daddy drove to Fairview Cemetery — the only time either of us went back to Jonas's grave that summer. Daddy called me at the NICU as he stood at the gravesite. It was

Jonas's gravesite

strange having that conversation, picturing Daddy on that lonely hilltop where one twin lay in a little concrete box, as I stood near your bedside where the other twin lay in a little plastic box.

Thursday, July 11, 2002

Daddy held you for the first time that night. You weren't used to being out of your incubator, and you kept blinking your sleepy, confused little eyes at Daddy as if to say, "Where am I?"

"I guess Hiram won't be able to do much," I remarked to Linda, who was caring for you. Daddy and I both secretly thought you might be normal, but we hesitated to say so. Most of the NICU staff seemed very cautious, almost pessimistic, when making predictions about your neurological outlook.

But Linda answered quickly, "Don't say that! Hiram could really surprise you with what he can do someday!"

I was so thankful to hear Linda say that. Her assertion gave me permission to be openly optimistic, to hope for the best, even while bracing for the worst.

Sunday, July 14, 2002

I met Daddy and Patience and Owen at Art and Lorinda's church. People were praying for us there because Lorinda had been updating her Sunday school class about you.

Patience and Owen were unruly even before church

began, and Lorinda graciously offered to take them to a nearby park. As she led them away, my heart melted at the thought of all they'd been through this summer. I decided I should be with them, and ran to catch up with Lorinda on her way to the park.

"I haven't seen them all week," I said. "I really need to be with them right now. You go back to church and I'll play with them at the park."

Patience and Owen's faces brightened. My face brightened too. I spent the whole hour playing and reconnecting with my older two children.

After the service, I took Patience and Owen back into the church. The visiting minister greeted us with a smile. He remembered me from high school days.

"So you have two children?" he asked us, glancing at Patience and Owen.

Daddy and I answered yes, we had two children; then we looked at each other as we remembered you. Since you never went anywhere with us, we sometimes forgot to count you.

"Well, actually, we have three children," Daddy tried again. "One of them is in the hospital."

Then we thought of Jonas. We looked at each other again.

"No . . ." Daddy slowly corrected himself one last time. "We have four children. One of them died." Daddy went on to explain about you and Jonas.

How many children do you have? That question still baffles me. Do I count Jonas? I don't like bringing death into a conversation when someone innocently asks how many children we have. Yet Jonas is my son too. I'll probably always struggle with that question.

Tuesday, July 16, 2002

E-mail:

In addition to praying for Hiram, we need prayers for us too, as we try to do what's best for our family. It's stressful for all of us to have the older children in Hershey; yet it's hard when we're not all together. There really aren't any good options — just a matter of choosing the option that does the least damage.

Patience and Owen need us, Hiram needs us, and we need each other. We've been married seven years and only once had we spent the night apart before last week. It wouldn't be so bad if it was a short-term problem. But we've already been in Hershey for seven and a half weeks and we don't expect to be able to bring Hiram home till October sometime; so we really need to figure out how we're going to do this. We all really miss each other. It feels almost like a divorce except that Russ and I love each other and want to be together. I really worry about the impact all this is having on Patience and Owen, so please pray along these lines for us.

Wendy

P.S. Hiram weighs over 3 pounds now.

Thursday, July 18, 2002

The whole family was together in Hershey again, and I brought Patience in to visit you. We arrived just after you'd had your diaper changed and your breathing tube suctioned and you were asleep.

Patience busied herself making a picture for you with colored pencils, and we posted it on the bulletin board at your bedside. This was the first of many pictures your big sister drew for you. By summer's end, you had a thick stack of artwork on your bulletin board.

Thursday, July 25, 2002

E-mail:

They weighed Hiram again last night and he's now 3 pounds 8.5 ounces. He has 1.5 ounces to go before he triples his birth weight.

Wendy

Sunday, July 28, 2002

At Light and Hope that morning, we started off with a very familiar song: "God is Good All the Time." *This must be their favorite song,* I thought. It seemed like we sang it every week.

I was uncomfortable speaking or singing those words without meaning them. The song chafed my conscience, forcing me to keep my heart right. I didn't get a week "off" to allow my attitudes to slip. This song reminded me weekly that God *is* good all the time. But was it good that God allowed Jonas to die?

Jim preached about giving up what you love, using the rich young man in Matthew, chapter 19, as an illustration.

We had given up what we loved: Jonas. But we hadn't been given a choice. Yet we *did* have a choice. We didn't choose to allow him to die, but we did choose how we responded to his death.

Part Three

We weren't angry with God, but we continued to deal with the frustration we felt toward my doctors. We needed to forgive them—even if they had ignored my concerns, even if they had been negligent, and even if they had cost Jonas his life. I'd forgiven them already—many times. And I would probably need to forgive them many times more. Every time I thought I'd won the battle and forgiven them once and for all, my sinful nature would rise up again—that old feeling of indignation and incredible frustration. I'd want to shake my doctors by the collar and ask, "What were you thinking?" But I had to continue forgiving.

Monday, July 29, 2002

I went to Dr. Buczewski about a pain on my right side just below my ribs, but he found nothing wrong. "It's probably musculoskeletal," he said, and gave me a list of symptoms to watch for.

"Why didn't you go to Dr. Rosato?" he asked.

"I don't really want to go back to my obstetricians until I have time to figure out how I feel about how they handled my pregnancy," I explained. I watched Dr. Buczewski's face for some reaction, to see if I could read any opinion about my obstetricians' competency. But his face remained completely neutral.

Thursday, August 1, 2002

I called Dr. Rosato's office and canceled the next day's postpartum checkup. Dr. Rosato later called my cell phone and asked about the cancellation. I explained that I'd

165

scheduled with an OB in Hershey because I didn't want to leave Hiram. That was true, but not the whole truth. Our lawyers had cautioned me not to give Dr. Rosato any clue that we were unhappy with the care I'd received from him.

Friday, August 2, 2002

While kangarooing you that evening, I noticed that the tape holding your breathing tube looked flimsy. Kathy was on duty, and I asked her to look at your tape. She thought it looked sturdy enough. A few minutes later, you whipped your little head back. I caught your head in time to keep you from flinging yourself out of my shirt, but not in time to keep your breathing tube from slipping out of your mouth. The tube had been anchored to my shirt and didn't move with your head. I suddenly saw an extra inch or so of breathing tube hanging out of your mouth.

"Uh . . . Kathy," I said, trying not to sound panicked, "I think Hiram just lost his breathing tube."

Kathy reached my side in one leap. She ripped you from my shirt, got you back in your isolette, and slapped an oxygen mask on your face. Someone summoned a respiratory therapist. I held the breathing tube so it wouldn't fall. A dirty breathing tube would either have to be replaced or wiped with alcohol, and I didn't want any delays getting you back on the ventilator. The respiratory therapist seemed surprised when I said I was your mother.

"I thought you were the resident," he said. "You were so calm."

Rather than reinserting the tube, the nurse practitioner

put you on CPAP — the same thing you'd had for about a day at Reading Hospital. I was glad she gave you a chance to breathe on your own, but it was awful to watch your little chest suck in as you struggled for every breath. I found myself breathing in sync with you, as though I could help you breathe.

You cried twice. We'd seen you cry before, but never heard you. While the breathing tube was between your vocal cords, it was impossible for you to make any noise. It had been pathetic to see your face scrunch up, and your mouth open wide to cry. But with the breathing tube out, I might be able to hear you.

I saw your little mouth open up to cry, and I quickly opened the isolette door and put my ear to the opening. Your cry was so faint that I could barely hear it, and it sounded like a faraway, newborn kitten. The sound was seared into my memory. I knew I might never hear it again.

I stayed by your side till around eleven, after the shift change. When I left, your nurse promised to call me if the breathing tube was reinserted.

I slept lightly that night, anticipating a call from the NICU. At 2:00 a.m., your nurse called to say that you'd had a really high CO_2 level, and they'd decided to put you back on the ventilator again.

I was relieved and slept soundly the rest of the night, knowing the ventilator was once again doing its familiar job.

Saturday, August 3, 2002

Until now, I'd given little thought to making you a baby

quilt. Daddy and I decided the time had come. I would start the quilt, believing you would come home someday to use it. I'd been working on a design for a few days, and we knew the amounts and varieties of fabrics I wanted. The quilt would have Ohio stars in shades of blue, green, and yellow set on a white background, with a checkered border running between the stars.

Sunday, August 4, 2002

You weighed just over 4 pounds now and were gaining well. Your ventilator settings continued to come down, and your lungs were improving. Yet we still wondered if you would ever come home. When Daddy or I asked the doctors what they thought your chances were for survival, they always said the same thing — 50 percent. That was a lot better than your original odds of less than 20 percent, but it reminded us you could still die.

Three babies in your corner of the NICU were about the same gestation and born around the same time — Kyra, Treasure, and you. Daddy used to call you three "the Bermuda Triangle," joking that when nurses went in they never came out. They ended up trapped among your isolettes, checking the numerous alarms you three babies made. Of the three, you seemed the most likely candidate to die. Kyra had no major health problems, and Treasure was doing much better than you.

Treasure had, in fact, been up to full feeds for a while now. Hector and Erica's three-hour commute from their home to Hershey really wore them out, so the Hershey doctors said they could take Treasure back to Scranton until her reconnect surgery. Hector and Erica were thrilled to be closer to home. As Hector and Erica packed their belongings and cleaned out their room at RMH, nine-year-old Joey, seven-year-old Kayla, and four-year-old Allie played with Patience and Owen on the playground.

"In a month or so my sister will be home with us," Joey said excitedly as he swung from the playground equipment. "I can't wait."

The end of their NICU summer was in sight, and I was so happy for them. Soon they'd all be home as a family. I wondered if we'd ever see that day with you.

Although I was happy for Hector and Erica, I had grown close to Erica and would sorely miss her. We had gone through so much together that she was like a sister to me. Erica seemed to sense this as she reassured me, "We'll be back. In a month or so we'll be back."

Chapter Twenty-Two

Saturday, August 10, 2002

Jeanne had transport duty again. She told me she would be going to Scranton to get Treasure. I gasped, and my legs felt shaky. *Why does Treasure need to come back here already?* I wondered. *She's been back at Scranton less than a week.* We'd grown so close to Hector and Erica that hearing bad news about Treasure was almost as awful as hearing bad news about you.

I made sure to be there when Treasure and her parents arrived. I didn't know why Treasure was coming back, but I knew it must be bad when Jeanne said to me, "Erica's really going to need you now."

When they arrived, Erica was distraught, and Hector wasn't doing much better. Erica said Treasure's belly had started swelling that morning, and they suspected another bout of NEC. Treasure had survived one round of that already. Could she survive another?

I'll never forget Erica pacing back and forth, taking big, agitated gulps of air, and chanting, "My baby can't die. My baby can't die. My baby can't die . . ."

From your bedside, I could see Treasure's shiny, distended belly protruding above the shallow sides of her warmer bed. I promised Erica I would e-mail everyone on my list an urgent request to pray for Treasure.

When I saw how poorly Treasure was doing, I began to worry about you. The doctors had faithfully warned us about everything that could go wrong, but no one had ever told us that you could get NEC again.

"Jeanne," I called, "does Hiram's belly look okay? It looks a little distended to me."

Jeanne came to inspect. "It looks fine to me," she said. "But I can call Dr. Mujsce over to look at it if you want."

Before I could respond, she called to Dr. Mujsce, who was only a few beds away: "Dennis? Can you take a look at Hiram's belly? His mom thinks it looks distended."

"Jeanne, it's okay," I said, embarrassed. "I'm sure it's fine . . . It's just after seeing Treasure come back looking like that . . ."

Jeanne's face melted in realization and sympathy. "I didn't even think about that."

"I didn't know babies could get NEC again," I said. "I'm just a little on edge."

Jeanne explained that a second bout of NEC is almost unheard of. Your belly seemed a lot smaller after Jeanne's reassurance.

Meanwhile, the neonatologists ordered X-rays of Treasure's belly and paged the surgeons. We all worried what the surgeons would find once they opened her up.

Less than a week before, Treasure's brother Joey had been anticipating her homecoming. Would that ever happen? We were crushed. You were doing great now in comparison to Treasure.

The NICU was closed for Treasure's surgery. Daddy and I saw Hector and Erica pacing at the far end of the hallway. Every now and then they peered through the windows of the NICU doors. Treasure's bed was located where they could see the surgeons' backs as they operated.

Daddy went and gave Hector a hug, saying, "Hector, sometimes a handshake just doesn't cut it."

I'd been doing a lot of thinking about thresholds lately. Treasure's condition made me think about it all the more. A threshold exists between death and life — a point at which a critical condition will lead to death. We see it all the time, like when someone is killed in a car accident. Would the victim have lived if he'd been traveling 10 mph slower? 15 mph slower? if he'd been a few seconds sooner or later?

I wondered how close you had come to dying. Or how close Jonas had come to living. How close had you both been to that threshold? At what point had it been too late to stop my labor? At what point could we have diagnosed and treated the TTTS? Would it have made any difference? Maybe you would have both lived. Or maybe you would have both died. Maybe we'd have Jonas and not you. How close had we been to those thresholds?

I pictured you and Jonas as two tiny raindrops falling side by side in the sky — almost touching each other. You landed at the continental divide — right at the threshold. Jonas went to one side, and you teetered on the edge for a long time before going down the opposite slope. After having begun so close together, you and Jonas find your-selves a world apart.

Now Treasure teetered on that threshold.

Sunday, August 11, 2002

E-mail:

Treasure came through surgery ok. A lot of dead bowel had to be taken out. She has just enough left that she can live. If there had been any less the doc would have just closed her back up and told her parents that they needed to pull the plug. The next few days will be really critical for her, so I appreciate all of your prayers.

Hiram is continuing to do well. He has an infection that he's getting antibiotics for, but they caught it early, so he's doing fine.

Wen

Saturday, August 24, 2002

Grandma spent Friday night and Saturday with me in Hershey. I showed Grandma your recently finished quilt top. When I'd begun assembling it, I had too many quilt blocks. I used the extra blocks to make a pretty back to your quilt. If Jonas had lived, I would have made two quilts anyway. It seemed appropriate to make your quilt double-sided.

Grandma left for home around 4:00 Saturday afternoon. Daddy and Patience and Owen wouldn't return till after 7:00. I had planned to walk to the hospital to visit you, but a thunderstorm blew up; and the shuttle bus had already made its last run for the day. So I had nothing to do.

Then I spied scraps left over from your quilt. Impulsively, I decided to make a small quilt for Jonas. Within twenty minutes, I had a small quilt top completed, just the size of his tiny body. I debated whether or not to put batting and a back on it. In the end, I decided to leave it unfinished — just like Jonas's life.

Monday, August 26, 2002

Today I had an appointment with Dr. Boyd Clary, the Hershey obstetrician. I brought a copy of my records with me.

A friendly nurse weighed me and asked, "So what did you have? a girl or a boy?"

"Two boys," I answered without really thinking about it.

"Oh! Twins!" she bubbled. "Who's watching them for you today?"

"Well, actually, one of them died and the other one is in the NICU. They were preemies." I reported this as emotionlessly as if I'd been giving a weather report.

The nurse's face instantly fell, and I could tell she wished she'd never asked — for my sake and hers.

Sometimes I could tell the story of you and Jonas so easily — no tears, just the facts; and other times, I would unexpectedly be reduced to weeping. That happened when I stepped into the exam room. Although it was a different doctor's office, it brought back a flood of memories. The last time I'd been in an OB/GYN office, you and Jonas had both been alive.

When Dr. Clary entered the room and began to take my OB history, I choked up with tears. He was very professional, but personal and compassionate. Physically, I was fine, but he wanted me to come back in four weeks to assess my risk for postpartum depression. I didn't know if I was at risk or not, but I felt that discussing with another OB the events leading up to your birth would be a boon to my mental health. I never did go to my follow-up appointment. When I got the appointment reminder in the mail, I saw that they'd scheduled me with a different doctor. How would a different doctor know if I seemed more depressed than I had last time?

Thursday, August 29, 2002

E-mail:

Hiram is still doing well. The rest of us are doing lousy. This has been the worst week yet for us all. The children aren't behaving; Russ and I are on edge. Hiram got moved to the other end of the NICU, so we don't even see the parents of our former NICU neighbors. They had become a sort of support network — and we don't have that now. We feel cut off from everyone. We could use some visits or phone calls or whatever. We need support. It's been over three months now and there is still no end in sight.

Wendy

You had been moved from bed number 18 to bed number 8. I didn't like bed number 8 at all. Bed number 18 had been in the rear corner of the unit, with very little traffic.

Also, I missed the nurses. But most of all, I missed the other parents. Bed number 18 had been near Treasure and Kyra.

The nurse manager was sympathetic and understanding when we asked if you could be moved back. But she explained that because of the many really sick babies at your end of the NICU, some of the more complicated babies like you had to be moved.

Back in our room, all Daddy could talk about was how the move had upset him. Meanwhile, an e-mail from Grandma mentioned a mysterious pain Grandpa had been experiencing in his arms. He could hardly keep up with all the work. I felt guilty as I pictured Grandpa mowing the yard and building home security products — all without our help.

"Do you think we should start going home once a week again to help out?" I asked Daddy.

"I can't believe they moved Hiram," Daddy answered.

"My dad's having a really hard time keeping up at home."

"Maybe if we talk to the nurse manager again we could get Hiram moved back."

"My parents said we could defer the rent, but maybe they're changing their minds . . ."

Then we realized we were each having our own conversation — and neither of us was listening to the other. By that time, we were upset with each other too. How bad were things going to get? We would soon see.

Later that evening, Elaine Spicher, a social worker who worked some evenings at the House, asked to talk to us. A lovely young mother with three small children of her own, she knew we'd been having trouble with Patience, and we welcomed the opportunity to talk to her.

Elaine tactfully suggested that we take the children home for a while to get them better disciplined. We appreciated the advice, but explained that we all needed to be together. As she continued to try to persuade us to take Patience and Owen home, a realization slowly dawned on us.

"Are you telling us," I asked, "that we *have* to take the children home?"

With sympathy and concern written across her face, Elaine nodded. Daddy and I could stay in our room, but the children were not welcome until they were better behaved.

As reality sank in, I began to cry. How much more could we be expected to take? Our world was shattering. Our family was going to be divided.

Daddy packed some essentials for Patience and Owen and took them home that night.

Chapter Twenty-Three

Friday, August 30, 2002

The "kick out" could hardly have come at a worse time. You'd spent the last two months in cycles of slow progress and abrupt setbacks, with no real gain. And then the morning after Patience and Owen left, you began one of your worst bouts of infection.

Back at the House I cleaned the children's things out of our room. It was amazing how much stuff had migrated from our home to our room at RMH.

As Hector and Erica saw me loading things into our van, they asked what had happened. When I explained, they were incredulous.

"Your children were the best in the House!" Hector exclaimed.

In a way he was right. Patience and Owen were always careful with the toys in the playroom and with other House property. They always treated other children kindly. In those ways they did well. But Hector and Erica had never seen Patience in a fit of crying and screaming when we tried to make her obey. In that way, our children (mostly Patience) did not behave well at all.

As the day went on it looked like your feeds weren't being digested. When a nurse drew back on the feeding tube at the start of a feeding, undigested milk would be drawn up. And this infection seemed particularly bad.

I wished Daddy and I could be together, but we couldn't. We had to take turns staying home with two unruly little children.

E-mail:

Russ is in Hershey with Hiram today, and I am at home with the children. Russ and I will just be taking turns with each other — kind of like a relay. Maybe soon we'll have Patience under control enough to all be up together in Hershey again. I know that when that time comes, we'll really be scrutinized to make sure that we're living up to the House's standards. So our bad week got even worse. I wonder how much stress any one family can take.

Wendy

Sunday, September 1, 2002

E-mail:

Hiram had his first physical therapy session on Friday. Pretty much all the therapist did was to assess him. He seems to have some motor impairment in his right arm which may turn out to be nothing or may be an early sign of cerebral palsy. The therapist left instructions on how to position Hiram in his crib so that he develops as normally as possible.

Hiram is getting a broviac line inserted today. He's running out of places to do IVs. The broviac is a surgically implanted line that goes into one of the main vessels near the heart.

Wendy

P.S. Keep praying for the rest of us too. This being apart is really wearying.

Friday, September 6, 2002, Hiram and Jonas's Due Date

E-mail:

Tomorrow Hiram will be 16 weeks old, and today is when Hiram and Jonas were due to be born. This gives me some perspective of just how early they were.

We'll be having a conference with the doctors and Hiram's nurse and the therapists to discuss our plan for Hiram for the upcoming weeks — like when to do surgery to reconnect his bowels, whether to keep giving him formula or start back on breast milk. I'll let you all know how that goes.

Wendy

Sunday, September 8, 2002

E-mail:

The children were here in Hershey last night and are staying again tonight. The Ronald McDonald House people said we could try them here a few days a week. It's very hard to be a good parent when I feel that I have to second-guess everything I do and wonder if it meets with others' approval.

Wendy

Part Three

Monday, September 9, 2002

Today we talked with your doctors about your reconnect surgery. A barium study several weeks before had pro-
vided some very good news: your "questionable" section of
bowel had healed itself—no blockages or perforations. After
your surgery, you'd have a normal-length bowel for absorb-
ing nutrients and water. Until then, you had a very short section; and your feeds had to be increased very slowly. With
the setbacks because of infections, you seldom got even a
third of your feeds through your stomach, which meant a lot
of your nutrition was IV.

But IV nutrition is very hard on the liver. And if they
reconnected your bowels, you'd temporarily take all your
feeds through the IV, but the amount of feeds could increase
more quickly, since you would have your whole bowel with
which to absorb nutrients. Ultimately, you'd be off the IVs
sooner if you had surgery. Weighing almost six pounds
now, you could tolerate the surgery. We agreed to go ahead.

Tuesday, September 10, 2002

Every other Tuesday, the hospital hosted a pizza dinner
for the NICU parents. It gave us a chance to visit with one of
the nurses, the patient advocate, and the other NICU parents. Patience and Owen always looked forward to the pizza
nights. We often had only two or three couples, but tonight
we had six.

We went around the table introducing ourselves and
telling briefly about our babies. Daddy and I told about
you, but not Jonas. I didn't want the other parents to feel

self-conscious sharing their stories once they knew how much we'd been through. But as the other parents told their stories, I began wishing we had told all of ours. Jonas was part of our story too.

The last couple to share had also had twins. The baby girl was here at Hershey, and the baby boy had died. A car had struck the mother when she was twenty weeks pregnant, and the boy's amniotic sac had leaked fluid after the impact. They'd held off delivery until twenty-seven weeks, but the boy had died at seven hours of age. Apparently, babies can exercise their lungs by "breathing" amniotic fluid. The boy's lungs had failed because he'd had no fluid to practice breathing with. I wondered then if the same thing would have happened to Jonas, even if we could have resuscitated him.

"You had twins too!" I exclaimed. Here was my chance to mention Jonas after all.

As Daddy and I swapped stories with them, a man with a smug, self-important air entered the room.

We assumed he was another NICU parent. He wasn't. He was a pastor who had gotten lost looking for a member of his congregation. We invited him to share some pizza with us anyway. When someone explained that we were parents of NICU patients, the man immediately looked interested.

"Would you like me to pray for any of your babies?" he asked. "I've prayed for a lot of sick people. I have a ninety percent success rate of healing people." He continued touting his record of the people "he" had healed. He gave no credit to God.

He gave Daddy and me the creeps.

He smiled convincingly at us, apparently oblivious to the parents' stony looks. All of us had sick babies. Two couples had a dead twin. And Treasure had just come back from Scranton.

Daddy and I had been talking a lot about what faith really is in a situation like ours. I could not leave this man unanswered. My heart hammered.

"Sir," I began, "you say if we have enough faith, our children will be healed. We had 100 percent faith that our twins would live. It didn't work. One of them died.

"Since then we've learned what faith really is. Faith isn't always believing that God will do just as we ask. Faith is also the confidence that, even if things don't go the way we want, someday we'll be able to say it was okay, that God had a good purpose in what He allowed. *That's faith.*"

I doubt my word swayed the man. I hope at least some of the other parents were reassured.

The man looked around the room again. This time the uncomfortable silence seemed to register.

"I guess my services aren't wanted here," he said. Then he left.

Wednesday, September 11, 2002

Your surgery was scheduled for Friday. In addition to the bowel surgery, the surgeons wanted to do a liver biopsy and a G-tube, which goes from outside the abdomen straight into the stomach. A G-tube is usually done for preemies with bad reflux, so that they can still be fed. You didn't have reflux.

But the surgeons wanted to insert it just in case you needed it in the future. Daddy and I hesitated. We wanted to be sure it was the best decision before we signed the consent forms.

We talked with Dr. Cheng, the chief surgery resident. She was wonderful. She knew the answers to all our questions and did an excellent job explaining things to us.

We expressed our hesitancy about the G-tube. She explained that you would probably need a G-tube at some point; and it was better to do it when you were already under general anesthesia. If you didn't get the G-tube, you could continue getting supplemental feedings through the tube that went through your nose and into your stomach, but its long-term use posed a greater risk of sinus problems. The biggest selling point for us was that you'd be able to learn to nurse better with the G-tube, because you could breathe through both nostrils.

After all you'd been through, the G-tube should not have been that big of a deal. But your belly had looked so weird for so long—first the Penrose drain, then the ostomy bag (not to mention the dressing when your incision had split open). We'd been looking forward to you having a normal belly, but now you'd come out of surgery with yet another piece of plastic attached to your abdomen. We had to ditch the idea of you having a "pretty" belly. After talking to Dr. Cheng, we signed the consent form.

Friday, September 13, 2002

In preparation for surgery, your nurse moved you from your crib to an open warmer bed. We stayed beside you, praying and waiting for the call from the OR. This would be your first surgery in the OR. The others had been done in the NICU because you'd been too sick to be moved.

We walked beside your bed as your nurse wheeled you out to the elevators, and then down to the second floor to the OR. This was a whole different world, with no pretense of décor—just stark, monochrome walls and no windows— only the artificial glow of fluorescent lights. It was quiet too—no voices, no echoes, no sounds of doors opening and closing. It seemed as though all the color and sound had been drained from this floor. Although the hallway was wide and well-lit, it felt narrow and claustrophobic. I felt as if we were in the very bowels of the hospital.

The anesthesiologist met us, and we watched as he wheeled your bed away; then we took the elevator to the first floor. Sounds and colors reappeared as we stepped off the elevator into the bustling traffic of employees and visitors coming and going from the cafeteria, the gift shop, and the administrative offices. It was hard to believe that the stark OR level was just above our heads.

After purchasing snacks, we returned to the elevators and the seventh floor to wait. After several hours someone from the NICU reported that the surgery was over. We caught a glimpse of you as a team of medical personnel pushed your bed purposefully down the hall on your way back to the NICU. We recognized Dr. Cheng and Dr. Dillon. Dr. Cheng smiled broadly and mouthed the words, "Everything is *okay!*"

Once they had delivered you to the NICU, Dr. Dillon

returned to talk to us. "The surgery went very well," he said. "We reconnected his bowels as planned, and gave him the G-tube. I also cleaned up a lot of scar tissue in there. I didn't do the liver biopsy because the liver didn't look that bad."

"How long until we can restart feeds?" we wanted to know.

"When Hiram has bowel sounds and begins passing stool, then we can restart feeds," Dr. Dillon explained. "That will probably take about two weeks. Even if it takes longer, don't be worried about it. Sometimes it takes awhile. Our main concerns for Hiram are possible infection, and we want to make sure his lungs aren't filling with fluid. He'll probably look sicker for the first week."

Chapter Twenty-Four

Saturday, September 14, 2002

The next morning you already had bowel sounds, amazing everyone. You were supposed to look *sicker* after your surgery. Your ventilator settings looked great too. You were turned back to 23 percent oxygen—just 2 percent above room air.

Later in the day, Mom Mom and Pop Pop brought Patience and Owen back to Hershey. Patience and Owen had behaved well for both sets of grandparents over the last several days, and we hoped they'd do as well for us at RMH. Maybe things were starting to improve for our family.

Sunday, September 15, 2002

A young Mennonite couple named Lyndon and Lynelle Martin came to RMH today. Their four-week-old daughter and only child was in the Pediatric Intensive Care Unit (PICU) because of a gastrointestinal ailment.

Now that your condition was so improved, Daddy and I had time to think about theological issues—mainly about the

Mennonites. This was interesting timing. I got to know Lynelle pretty well.

"I used to have the same convictions as you do when I was in high school," I told Lynelle. I didn't know how she would respond, but I went on anyway. "I used to wear a covering and dresses, but once I graduated I got away from it. Russ and I are really considering a lot of those things again."

"I noticed that you usually wear a dress," Lynelle commented.

No condemnation — no questioning why I had turned my back on convictions she firmly adhered to. She simply promised to pray for me as a sister in the Lord as we sought out what God's Word said about different things.

Monday, September 16, 2002

An Amish couple with five children had also been staying at RMH. People tried to befriend them. I held back at first, but that changed after a brief conversation with the husband. He happened to be sitting in the living room when Patience and I came in. He had a very friendly, approachable manner.

"So which one of your children is in the hospital?" I asked. Anywhere else, this would be a pretty heavy topic; but in Hershey, this is small talk.

"Jesse Alan," he replied. "He's seven years old."

"What happened?" More Hershey-style small talk.

"He fell out of the hay hole in his grandparents' barn. He has a head injury."

"How's he doing?"

"He had some brain swelling at first, but it seems to be getting a lot better now."

I nodded in silent sympathy, and then explained why we were there. "We always wanted a larger family," I explained. "It seemed like we were getting a jump on things with twins, but now…" I let that thought dangle, and then changed the subject: "I don't think I got your names."

"Sam and Susan Stoltzfus."

"Russ and Wendy Boyd."

We talked a little more, and then Sam stated the obvious: "A lot of people have been trying to befriend my wife, and they're nice ladies and everything … "

His next words really surprised me, "But someone like you . . . I think my wife would really enjoy getting to know someone like you."

Someone like me? I glanced at my button-down blouse and long, full denim skirt. Maybe I looked more conservative than I realized. I took some opportunities to get acquainted with Susan. Sam was right. We really did enjoy each other's company.

Once I took Susan in to see you. Sam waited in the hallway outside the scrub room. As he observed us doing the required two-minute scrub, he called good-naturedly, "Are you two getting a shower in there or something?"

Susan and I laughed. The two-minute scrub could seem like overkill to the uninitiated.

After Jesse had been moved from the PICU to the rehab floor, Susan invited me to one of his physical therapy sessions. He was recovering remarkably well from his brain injury. I kept Nathan, their eight-month-old, occupied at one end of the therapy room so she could be involved in Jesse's therapy.

We visited a lot throughout the rest of Jesse's hospital stay.

Tuesday, September 17, 2002

E-mail:

Hiram has been doing great since surgery. The docs had all been warning us that he would initially look sicker after surgery, but so far he's been looking great. He's not puffed up or anything.

If he is still looking this good tomorrow, we're going to start weaning his vent settings with the hope of getting him off the ventilator sometime in the next few weeks.

Amazingly, Hiram had bowel sounds already on Saturday morning, plus he had three bowel movements yesterday and one so far today. They haven't started feeding him even though he's met their criteria because they want the bowel to be more healed at the reconnection site before putting anything in there.

Obviously, they weren't expecting this much progress this soon! I think if all continues to go well, they may start feeds Friday. We'll see.

Thank you all for praying for Hiram. I don't think he'd be doing even half this well if it weren't for you all.

Wendy

Wednesday, September 18, 2002

Lyndon and Lynelle went home with their daughter. I

was glad to see them resume normal life, but I wished I'd had time to get to know them better. Our lives had intersected for such a brief time.

I was surprised when I saw that she had left her address for me, asking if I would be interested in corresponding with her. Her scribbled note said she just couldn't leave without saying good-bye.

Thursday, September 19, 2002

While we were home, your nurse Linda called to tell us your tube had come out. At shift change, your previous nurse had been reporting to Linda when they heard crying from your crib. They went to investigate, and there you were, holding your breathing tube in your hand. Dr. Javier told me later that when she ran toward your crib, she met Linda running the other direction.

"Where are you going?" Dr. Javier exclaimed.

"I have to get the camera!" Linda called over her shoulder.

Once Dr. Javier got to your crib, she understood. You were breathing well on your own. Since your medical safety wasn't at stake, the nurse wanted to snap a picture of this milestone.

Linda felt sure you'd do well off the ventilator this time. She was Treasure's primary nurse, so we'd gotten to know her well and respected her opinion.

When we returned to Hershey, you were breathing effortlessly. I could see what Linda meant. Unlike the last time you'd lost your tube, we felt very relaxed. You looked like you'd been breathing on your own all your life.

You still had some plastic tubing that wafted extra oxygen into your nose through two loose-fitting prongs. Although you could now handle the mechanics of breathing, you still needed the extra oxygen as your lungs healed from four months spent on the ventilator.

Although the surgeons had been planning on starting feeds today, they decided to wait until the next day. Being removed from the breathing tube was enough progress for one day.

Friday, September 20, 2002

I stared idly out the dining room window at RMH as Daddy and I ate breakfast with Patience and Owen. Occasionally House guests walked by the sidewalk that passed the dining room. I did a double take as I noticed a very familiar couple hurrying up the walk to the front door.

"It's Lyndon and Lynelle!" I exclaimed.

They had obviously come for a room and not for a social call, since they didn't have their baby. I ran to open the door for them.

"What are you doing back here?" I asked. "What's wrong with Jenni Lynn?"

"Once we had Jenni home, she went right back to being sick again," Lynelle explained. "So we were told to bring her back to Hershey. I hope we can really find out what's wrong this time."

I was glad to see them again, but so sorry that their baby was sick again.

Part Three

Saturday, September 21, 2002

Tom and Jill Whitmore and their two children came to visit us. They had been members of our fledgling church, Stone Hill Fellowship, but had left for another church a month or so before. As we ate, they chatted to us about the new church they were attending and other bits of news.

"I'm not sure if Pastor Dean has found another church since he shut down Stone Hill," Tom mentioned.

Our heads snapped up in surprise. "Dean did *what!?*" Daddy exclaimed.

"We thought you knew . . ." Tom looked embarrassed. He and Jill are *not* gossipy people. Of course he thought we'd know. Daddy was the assistant pastor.

We'd had little contact with Dean or with Stone Hill after you were transferred to Hershey. Now we discovered that we weren't only out of contact, we didn't even *have* a home church. I walked around in a daze the rest of that day.

Monday, September 23, 2002

I nursed you for the first time today. The nurse had me pump thoroughly first so you wouldn't get a lot of milk in your mouth and not know what to do with it. They call this non-nutritive sucking. I saw milk dripping out the corner of your mouth and down your cheek, so I knew you were getting a little bit anyway.

You were a natural at nursing. You swallowed the milk, while most babies with your history would have sputtered and gagged. It was good to see you enjoyed nursing. Many babies who've had a breathing tube in for a long time don't like having anything in their mouths.

The only thing we had to do before your discharge was to get you up to full feeds. We went from having no end in sight to realistically expecting to have you home in a couple of weeks.

We had you out of the NICU for a few hours for the first time today. Your nurse took you and your IV stand, and Daddy and me, over to the parents' rooming-in room. It had a sofa, a rocking chair, an attached bathroom, and an oxygen hookup. We enjoyed spending time with you in a normal setting.

Sam and Susan Stoltzfus took Jesse home. Like Lynelle, Susan left her address so we could write to each other. Lyndon and Lynelle left with their daughter a few days after that. They had finally pinpointed Jenni Lynn's problem. After putting her on special formula, she was fine.

It was a lot easier seeing other RMH parents go home now that we knew our day was coming soon. The hard part now was thinking about the families we would be leaving behind—especially Hector and Erica, who had no end in sight. Treasure was surviving, but not improving.

Tuesday, September 24, 2002

Daddy and I took you to the rooming-in room again, this time with Patience and Owen. Daddy shot some video while I sat with you on the sofa and Patience and Owen played. This was such a pleasant taste of what life would be like once you came home.

I nursed you again today. When I added up the ounces I pumped per day and compared it to the amount of milk a baby your size needed, it was enough for three of you. It tore at my heart when I saw those numbers. There would have been more than enough for both you and Jonas.

Though the milk supply was more than adequate, you tired easily. The doctors worried that you would stop nursing before you got enough. One of the tricky things about nursing a baby with a weak suck is guessing how many ounces he has nursed. The first time one of the doctors asked me how much milk I thought you had taken, I was bewildered. How did I know? But after a few days of nursing, I was feeling more confident about my ability to estimate.

When your nurse, Kelly, came to check on us, she had a syringe with extra milk. The resident thought you wouldn't have gotten enough and wanted to supplement with a little extra through your G-tube.

"He seemed to nurse really well," I told Kelly. "Do we have to supplement? I'm afraid we'll overfill him and make him spit up if we give him any more."

Kelly agreed with me. "He's nursing like a newborn back there!" she said to the resident.

"If the resident insists that Hiram needs more milk, tell him his mother refused," I added.

Chapter Twenty-Five

The weeks after your surgery passed in a whirlwind. We had grown accustomed to slow progress and fast setbacks; now you were progressing quickly. We went from wondering if you would survive to planning for your discharge.

We were thrilled that you would soon come home, but part of me felt panicky. I thought I'd have more time — more warning — to prepare to leave this place. Strange as it may sound, the hospital and RMH had come to feel like home and the NICU nurses like family. At home there would be no nurses to talk to every day, no Hector and Erica to visit with, no doctors to answer our every question about you. Even the hospital itself seemed to pulse and throb with energy; and we would be away from all that. We'd chosen Dr. Javier for your follow-up neonatologist. We'd still see her at the clinic, but it wouldn't be the same.

I spent almost all my time with you in the NICU. Now that you were nursing, I needed to be there. I also wanted to be there for you if you cried and needed to be held. Getting home would make this part easier. In the NICU if you had a crying spell, I was stuck until you calmed down. I couldn't go anywhere or do anything else. At home, I could read to Patience and Owen, or at least walk around our apartment while I held you.

Sunday, Sept. 30, 2002

We set a discharge date for the following Sunday, October 6. You would come home on oxygen and a monitor and lots of meds, and you would probably still be taking most of your feeds through the G-tube, but you'd be home.

We knew that would be a busy day, so this was our last Sunday at Light and Hope. The four of us said our good-byes to everyone. We would especially miss Pastor Jim, and Art and Nancy Husson.

After church, Daddy and I began cleaning our remaining belongings out of our room at RMH, leaving only what I would need that final week. Daddy spent that week at home with Patience and Owen. I spent my days at your crib side.

Now that the uncertainty of your survival was past, I felt that I was "thawing" spiritually. I could pray for specific things again. I prayed for strength for the parting from Hershey — especially since I was spending more time here when I felt I should be disconnecting.

Saturday, October 5, 2002

Daddy and I spent Saturday together in Hershey. We cleaned our room, leaving as little as possible to be done the next morning.

I knew I'd miss Hector and Erica most of all. I hated

leaving them with no end in sight for Treasure. They surprised us with a "coming home" gift for you — a musical bear.

Daddy went home that night to get some last-minute things ready for your homecoming.

Sunday, October 6, 2002

This was the day we had been working toward — the goal of the entire summer. I should have felt nothing but delight. Yet I knew I'd also be homesick for Hershey. And more significant, I knew I'd miss Jonas. There would be no more ups and downs, no more medical reports, and no other parents to visit with to distract me from grieving over Jonas.

I packed my small bag, finished cleaning our room and bathroom, and checked out with the weekend manager. I took one last look around the empty room that had been

Hiram with his parents

home for four months, and then walked out and shut the door.

I was near tears as I visited with you and Jeanne at the hospital. When Jeanne took your hospital "newborn" picture, I tried to explain. "It's so hard to be taking Hiram home without Jonas," I whispered, trying to hold back the tears. "It didn't really seem real this summer that we don't have Jonas, because we really didn't have Hiram either."

Jeanne seemed puzzled, so I explained further. "Hiram never went anywhere with us or did anything with us. It didn't seem like he was really part of the family yet. He was always here in the NICU."

Jeanne's understanding melted my defense against the tears.

"Every time Hiram reaches another milestone, I feel like we're leaving Jonas farther and farther behind," I sobbed. How could we take you home without Jonas?

Jeanne waited a moment before answering. Then she said, "But you know, he isn't really left behind."

I nodded. I knew what she meant. In a way, Jonas was up ahead, waiting for us to join him in Heaven. But that still didn't make today easier. I couldn't get past today's homecoming—today's *half* of a homecoming.

When she had taken your picture, Jeanne said I could stay in the crib room as long as I needed while she took you back to the NICU. Every time I thought I was ready to venture out to your bedside, a fresh flood of tears overwhelmed me. I was getting annoyed with myself. I wanted to be by your side to soak up the last few hours of your

NICU stay, but here I sat squandering my time bawling in the crib room.

After an hour or so, I walked resolutely out to your bedside. I would *not* cry.

Daddy arrived around 2:00 p.m. to take us home. We packed up your things, being careful not to leave anything behind. Into your bag went your clothes. Into your box went the pictures of Patience and Owen that we'd taped to your crib. We packed the drawings Patience had made for you, and the beanie babies you'd accumulated. We packed the Bible we'd kept at your bedside. Then Daddy took your things out to the van and made one last trip to the cafeteria to get us something to eat on the way home.

By 3:00 p.m. we had nothing left to do. It was time to go. All that was left was you, your car seat, your oxygen, and your monitor. We buckled you into your car seat and tucked your NICU blanket over you. Jeanne took a Polaroid of you in your car seat — another success story to add to their scrapbook. Then she announced to the other nurses: "Okay, everybody! Hiram's leaving now if anyone wants to come see him before he goes."

I felt my composure slipping, and hoped the nurses would be quick. I pasted a smile on my face as the nurses took one last look at you, and Jeanne escorted us down the elevator and out to our van. I climbed in first to the middle bench seat, and then we locked your seat into its base next to me. I handed the NICU blanket back to Jeanne, to be washed and used for another baby.

"You keep it," Jeanne said. "People make these things

for the babies to keep." The blanket would be another souvenir of your NICU stay.

We thanked Jeanne, and she wished us well. Then we drove off. As soon as we were out of sight, I let my tears flow. Daddy wasn't moved to tears like I was, but he understood. I knew I had over an hour to cry and talk to Daddy and cry some more before we arrived home.

As thankful as we were to have you home, we couldn't look at you without seeing Jonas. You were only half of the story. This brought me back to the same question I asked in the first paragraph of the first chapter of this book: Who left whom behind? You came home without Jonas. Jonas went Home without you.

Yet God sustained us in our grief. After the first difficult day, your first months at home were a very joyful, peaceful time. I continued to get up around 4:00 a.m. — not to visit you anymore, but to visit God. I would read some Scripture, pray for strength for the day, and then go back to sleep until around seven. I believe this time alone with my Savior made all the difference in those first weeks. We still grieved and shed tears, but it wasn't an overwhelming, all-consuming grief.

* * * * * * * *

About two weeks after you came home we sent out birth announcements. I had agonized over the wording, wanting to include Jonas, but wanting to do it tactfully. We put a picture of you on the outside of the announcement. On the inside we put a picture of you at two weeks old, along with a picture of Jonas. Opposite the pictures, I typed:

Born May 18, 2002

Due September 6, 2002

Identical twin sons of Russell and Wendy Boyd

Hiram Joseph Boyd

Born at 6:13 am

11 inches

1 lb. 3½ ounces

Came home to be with Mommy and Daddy

and Patience and Owen, October 6, 2002.

Jonas Nathaniel Boyd

Born at 6:15 am

11 inches

1 lb. 1 ounce

Went home to be with Jesus, May 18, 2002.

* * * * * * * * *

Daddy and I never asked ourselves, "Why me?" Why *not* us? Bad things happen to people all the time. Why should we be exempt? "Shall we indeed accept good from God and not adversity?" (Job 2:10) Job's experience was much worse than ours, yet he was faithful.

Although we never blamed God, I felt a little sorry for myself until a friend said to me, "Wendy, you are so blessed."

I wondered if I'd heard her right. *Blessed?* One of my children had died. But after thinking about it, I realized she was right. We *were* blessed. We had three healthy children

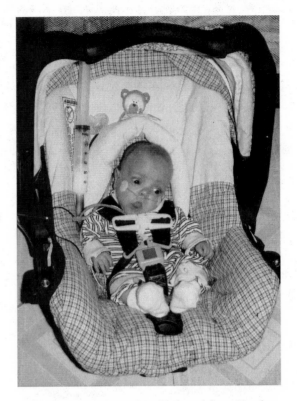

5-month-old Hiram after discharge from Hershey

and the promise of seeing Jonas again someday.

So I guess you could say that we have asked, "Why me?" We look at all our blessings and think, "Why me?"

I still have my dark days, like the day we moved you from your crib to the bottom bunk of the bed we'd bought for you and Jonas and Owen. You looked so lost all by yourself on that full-sized mattress. I shed tears as I both tried, and tried not, to picture another little boy who looked just like you sleeping in the empty space beside you. We still grieve, but not as those who have no hope. See 1 Thessalonians 4:13.

In closing, I'd like to share with you the words of what has become my favorite hymn. In the year 1873, an American named Horatio Spafford learned that all four of his children had perished at sea on a voyage to England with their mother. He immediately sailed for England to join his grieving wife. On his voyage, the captain told Mr. Spafford when they reached the approximate place where his children had died. There Mr. Spafford penned these words:

When peace, like a river, attendeth my way,
When sorrows, like sea billows roll;
Whatever my lot, Thou hast taught me to say,
"It is well, it is well with my soul."

Though Satan should buffet, though trials should come,
Let this blest assurance control,
That Christ hath regarded my helpless estate,
And hath shed His own blood for my soul.

My sin — Oh the bliss of this glorious thought —
My sin — not in part, but the whole,
Is nailed to His cross and I bear it no more —
Praise the Lord, praise the Lord, Oh my soul!

O Lord, haste the day when my faith shall be sight,
The clouds be rolled back as a scroll,
The trump shall resound, and the Lord shall descend,
"Even so," It is well with my soul.

Epilogue

Bringing home a preemie was a very different experience — not only for us, but also for Patience and Owen. About a month after Hiram's homecoming, Patience and Owen were sitting on the living room floor playing with their teddy bears. They both had a drinking straw, a tissue, and some tape on the bears' bellies. When I asked what they were doing, Patience replied with a big smile, "We're changing our bears' G-tube dressings." They didn't even know what it was like to have a typical newborn in the house. To them, changing a G-tube dressing was as normal as changing a diaper.

At every visit with Dr. Javier we asked if they could tell how Hiram would develop. Dr. Javier and the physical therapist would always answer carefully, explaining what they could without making any promises. They assured us that the older Hiram got, the better they could predict his eventual outcome.

As Hiram grew, they kept ruling out more and more of the bad end of the disabilities spectrum. Hiram continued

Hiram at 5 years old

to acquire skills.

When Hiram stopped using his right arm for a few days, we took him to see a neurologist who diagnosed him as having very mild cerebral palsy.

When I heard the words "cerebral palsy," I felt like someone had kicked me in the back of the knees. But the neurologist assured us that cerebral palsy is a broad term. For Hiram, it just means that he is a bit weak, stiff, and uncoordinated in his right side. The casual observer seldom notices. People are often puzzled when I mention the physical and occupational therapy that Hiram continues to get to maximize his abilities. They wonder why he needs it.

Hiram was very delayed with most of his skills. He sat independently at age fifteen months, crawled at age two, and walked before three. He started running and jumping at four.

Mentally he is fine. His speech was delayed initially. He had only about fifty words by age two and a half. But he has caught up since and is quite a communicator. At age five, he's learning to count and to recognize and write some letters. Everyone, from Hiram's neurologist to his therapists, has said that Hiram is a miracle. They say they have never seen any child with a medical history like Hiram's who looks as good as he does.

We are very blessed.

Patience and Owen blossomed into very well-behaved children who love Jesus. We continued to seek God, tried to be loving and consistent with our children, and began having family devotions every night.

Treasure Gonzales departed this life in the Hershey NICU on Feb. 8, 2003, at the age of eight months and four days. We still stay in contact with her parents

That first winter we didn't go to any church, because we had been cautioned to keep Hiram away from other people and their germs.

Over the following summer we visited several different churches, finally settling on a Mennonite church. Our biggest issue was whether or not a Christian woman should wear a head covering. I felt I couldn't make an unbiased decision, so I left it totally up to Russ. In April 2004, after much soul searching and study of 1 Corinthians 11, Russ decided I should wear a veil. We joined the church on my 29th birthday in June 2005.

Right around Hiram's first birthday (an extremely difficult time for us anyway), our lawyers finally gave us an answer. The perinatologist who reviewed my records said that since TTTS diagnosed at that gestation period has an almost 100 percent mortality rate, the outcome would likely not have been better even if it had been diagnosed earlier. We had no grounds for a lawsuit.

We were relieved. We had a growing conviction that Christians should not sue. We didn't want the money anyway; we just wanted answers.

During the week of Hiram's first birthday, we spent at least an hour with Dr. Rosato and Dr. Davis at their office, and Dr. Neubert and Dr. Brown at Reading Hospital — at no charge. What a flood of memories it brought back for us — the same doctors, the same hospital, the same time of year.

They explained the challenges of diagnosing and treating TTTS, rehearsed precautions taken, and told us of some cases similar to ours, also with disappointing results. We came away with a new respect for our doctors.

We went back to Dr. Rosato and Dr. Davis for the birth of our next child. Quentin Samuel Boyd was born on January 12, 2005. He was healthy, and only ten days early. Dr. Davis delivered him. Quentin means "the fifth child." Samuel means "asked of God."

A healthy sister, Melora Violet Boyd, joined the family

on July 5, 2007. When the midwife examined the placenta, she saw a rare defect that could easily have torn Melora's umbilical cord and caused her to bleed to death. The midwife called Melora "a miracle baby." We are so thankful that God let us keep her.

IF YOU WANT TO KNOW THE LIVING CHRIST

SEE Your Condition

"There is NONE RIGHTEOUS, no, not one. ALL HAVE SINNED" (Romans 3:10, 23).

"ALL we like sheep have GONE ASTRAY" (Isaiah 53:6).

HEAR God's Offer

"Believe on the Lord Jesus Christ, and THOU SHALT BE SAVED" (Acts 16:31).

"Incline your ear, and come unto me: hear, and YOUR SOUL SHALL LIVE; and I will make an everlasting covenant with you" (Isaiah 55:3).

TASTE God's Provision

"Blessed are they which do hunger and thirst after righteousness: FOR THEY SHALL BE FILLED" (Matthew 5:6).

"Jesus said unto them, I am the bread of life: he that cometh to ME SHALL NEVER HUNGER; and he that believeth on me SHALL NEVER THIRST" (John 6:35).

FEEL God's Transforming Power

"A new heart also will I give you, and a new spirit will I put within you: and I will take away the stony heart out of your flesh, and I will give you an heart of flesh" (Ezekiel 36:26).

LIVE in Newness of Life

Jesus said, "I am come THAT THEY MIGHT HAVE LIFE, and that they might have it MORE ABUNDANTLY" (John 10:10).

"As Christ was raised up from the dead by the glory of the Father, even so we also should walk in NEWNESS OF LIFE" (Romans 6:4).

Christian Light Publications, Inc., is a nonprofit, conservative Mennonite publishing company providing Christ-centered, Biblical literature including books, Gospel tracts, Sunday school materials, summer Bible school materials, and a full curriculum for Christian day schools and homeschools. Though produced primarily in English, some books, tracts, and school materials are also available in Spanish.

For more information about the ministry of CLP or its publications, or for spiritual help, please contact us at:

Christian Light Publications, Inc.
P. O. Box 1212
Harrisonburg, VA 22803-1212

Telephone—540-434-0768
Fax—540-433-8896
E-mail—info@clp.org
www.clp.org